Finding Faith

Finding Faith

STORIES OF MUSIC AND LIFE

Nick Baines

SAINT ANDREW PRESS
Edinburgh

First published in 2008 by
SAINT ANDREW PRESS
121 George Street
Edinburgh EH2 4YN

ISBN 978 0 7152 0868 7

British Library Cataloguing in Publication Data
A catalogue record for this book is available from the British Library

Typeset by Waverley Typesetters, Fakenham
Printed and bound by Bell & Bain Ltd, Glasgow

CONTENTS

CONTENTS

PROLOGUE

Over the last few years I have frequently been asked about my own life story and how I have ended up thinking, speaking and writing the way I do. I cannot imagine why anyone would be interested in my own story because it isn't very interesting in itself. Everyone has their own life and we just get on and live it, taking the opportunities offered up as we go. Most of us have no idea what lies ahead of us, but we order our memory in such a way as to try to give shape to what lies behind us. It is inevitable that we also impute to past decisions and events an order or intentionality that probably wasn't actually there. But, this does not matter a great deal in the grand scheme of things.

I cannot write a book that simply sets out to tell my own story. I wouldn't know where to start and, anyway, it certainly hasn't finished yet. Each turn in a life's course sheds new light on earlier events and experiences and I am wary of writing anything that might imply I have now got it all sorted out. I also don't think it would be very interesting as most of life is ordinary and unspectacular. So, I don't make any great claims to unique knowledge or experience; I just use certain experiences to illustrate what emerges from one particular life.

I love music and have found some of my favourite songs suggest a way into thinking about God, the world and me. There are many hundreds of songs I could have chosen, so any choice is somewhat arbitrary. I could, for example, have made sure I got a balance of male and female artists and could have attempted to prove my 'trendy' credentials by pretending (as some misguided politicians have done) to have an affinity for the Arctic Monkeys. I like the Arctic Monkeys, Kaiser Chiefs, Killers, Keane and lots of other bands, but they haven't shaped my life over the years.

Furthermore, I do not pretend to be an expert on the songs or the musicians – all I claim is that these songs have made me reflect on God, the universe and life. If the ten songs form a motley collection, so do the bits of my story I share in these pages. Inevitably, there are other songs, other stories and lots more that could be said. But, I want this simple book to be accessible and of interest to anyone who is interested in why other people believe what they do and live the way they do. This is also the reason several stories are alluded to more than once in the course of the book: each chapter can stand on its own as well as form part of a narrative.

In brief, I was born and grew up in Liverpool, went to university (German and French) in Bradford, worked as a professional linguist (Russian) for the British Government in Cheltenham, and am married with three adult children (two of them also now married). I have lived and worked for short periods of time in Germany, Austria and France. I served a curacy in the Lake District and then parishes in Leicestershire. We moved to London in 2000 when I was appointed Archdeacon of Lambeth and then to Croydon (ten miles south of

London) when I was consecrated Bishop of Croydon at St Paul's Cathedral in May 2003. I spent ten years on the General Synod of the Church of England and have served as a non-executive director of the Ecclesiastical Insurance Group. I have been involved in broadcasting and media in various ways for many years and have written several books. I am a musician and support Liverpool Football Club. That's it really.

But between those bare bones there are fifty years of experiences and hundreds of people who have shaped me and influenced my life. There have been successes and failures – I suspect more of the latter than the former.

And all through this life there has been the trace of God. I cannot pretend that this rumour of God has been always strong and incontrovertible; but, equally, I have never been able to shake it off. There have been many times when I have wished I could. Now, that might sound an odd or surprising thing for a bishop to say, but it shouldn't be; after all, I am called to tell the truth about God, the world and us. So, there is no point in pretending that things are what they are not. There have been times when God has seemed absent or, at best, distant. There have been times when I wished he would become more distant and even disappear completely. And there have been other times when I have experienced the intimacy of God's presence and touch in ways that cannot be described in mere words. But I have to be honest and say that there has been more 'absence' than 'intimacy' over all.

So, why am I a Christian? The answer lies in the conviction that God has revealed himself in Jesus and that this same Jesus has invited ordinary people like me to walk with him and learn to see through his eyes. So, I would be a Christian whether or not I 'feel' anything. Yes, this is an intellectual conviction, but it is more than that – and, unable to shake it off, I have embraced it as the defining feature of my life and the way I see the world. This book simply tells some stories about how I have found and continue to find faith in the God who has shown himself among us in Jesus of Nazareth.

Or does it? I think I have learned over the years that I haven't found faith and haven't found God: rather, God has found me and faith is the expression of that experience and my response to God. It comes as a great relief to note that when Adam and Eve mess up the creation in the Genesis narrative, it is not they who go looking for God, but God who comes looking for them. So, I could speak of the Christian journey as being the discovery in diverse ways that God has found me and opened my eyes to his love and generosity.

I am hugely grateful to so many people who have created the space in which I have found myself to be found by God. Not only my family, but all the innumerable people I have encountered during the years. They are too numerous to mention by name, but I want to acknowledge the immeasurable privilege of serving communities in Kendal, Rothley, and the Diocese of Southwark – especially the wonderful clergy and people of the Croydon Episcopal Area. I owe a huge debt to longstanding friends in Germany (Klimmeks and Semraus) and Austria (Türkis and Klaffenböcks). Silke Römhild read the initial script and her critique was helpful and full of wisdom. I am more grateful than I can say for friendships with colleagues, friends in so many places and especially those who have never given up on me.

This book is dedicated to Jonathan and Sue, Daphne and Roberto, Paul and Cathy – all of whom have shaped the journey written about in this book. But my greatest gratitude goes to Linda, Richard and Emma, Melanie and Liam, and Andrew.

Chapter 1

PENNY LANE

One of the great mysteries of human civilisation is how on earth little Jimmy Osmond ever got to sing *Long-haired Lover from Liverpool* when he had never been to the city, was too young to be a lover and had a bad haircut. I am from Liverpool, fell in love there (at the docks, to be precise) and had such a bad haircut throughout my youth that I can hardly bear to look at the photographs. Don't even think of mentioning the flared yellow trousers, the platform boots and the orange flared jacket. And now, with my credibility crushed, please read on.

Liverpool was a great city to grow up in during the 1960s and 1970s. It was vibrant with music, poetry, the arts and comedy. And although many famous names came from this cosmopolitan port city on the north-west coast of England, one name stands above all. Mention the Beatles anywhere in the world and you will get smiles of recognition and the humming of a tune. The Fab Four provided more than the backdrop to my early childhood and I still remember the excitement when yet another Beatles single was about to be released.

There was great pride around, even in children like me. The walk to primary school in the suburb where

I lived with my parents, two brothers and two sisters, was often accompanied by the swapping of little Beatles cards that we collected from sweet cigarette packets or magazines. Liverpool seemed to be bursting with creative and musical talent, with groups springing up everywhere and poets making the country laugh. The so-called Mersey Sound seemed to be ubiquitous: Gerry and the Pacemakers blessed the world not only with epic songs like *Ferry Cross the Mersey*, but also that great global football anthem that belongs to the Kop at Anfield, *You'll Never Walk Alone*.

Of course, it is always easier to look back on childhood with romantic eyes, but the 1960s were full of optimism as England emerged from the years of postwar austerity. With Elvis Presley shaping the new world of rock 'n' roll from the USA and the Rolling Stones competing with the Beatles for the passions of British youth, it was the four Scousers who (to my mind, at least) eventually emerged as the voice of a generation of young people escaping the hard years and opening up the possibility of a new future.

The world was changing rapidly during this decade and the subsequent legacy of the 1960s contains both good and bad elements. The sense of optimism was palpable, but the way it was expressed by architects in concrete in some English cities was (as seen thirty years later) both a community disaster and a design catastrophe. But while Berlin was being divided (on 13 August 1961) the Americans were planning to put a man on the moon (20 July 1969). The Civil Rights Movement in the USA was challenging the prejudices and injustices of the 'Land of the Free' while the superpowers appeared to be dividing Europe for ever.

Change brings energy – and there was plenty of that in the 1960s.

Yet optimism about a future free of conflict (despite the sniff of a Cold War and the threat of a nuclear stand-off) was expressed in terms of economic satisfaction and freedom in relationships. The so-called 'permissive society' was growing alongside the recognition of the need for civil rights on both sides of the Atlantic. As the British Empire continued its retreat, America continued to assert its growing confidence and might. African countries were challenging the yoke of colonial exploitation at the same time as western involvement in South-East Asia (Vietnam, Cambodia, etc.) began to look seriously misguided. The early promise of the Kennedy presidency lay bloodied in Dallas while the dream of landing a man on the moon was being pursued with vigour. In other words, optimism about a golden future marched hand in hand with fear about the human propensity to get it wrong in a fragile world – emerging from one global conflict just in time to threaten new and more catastrophic wars. Freedom was the heart-cry of Martin Luther King and those who decided that a new world was possible, but the whole of the globe was undergoing a radical movement of its intellectual, economic, social and emotional tectonic plates.

This is the world I was born into in 1957 in Liverpool, England. My earliest memories involve such romantic fantasies as permanent blue skies in the summer, deep snow all winter and babies coming along as regularly as the buses. I was born the second of five children to parents who had been born and bred in Liverpool and whose pride of place was inevitably going to rub off on the offspring. As I grew up I couldn't imagine how sadly impoverished people must be to grow up somewhere other than the place I knew to be 'home'. Liverpool was the heart of the world and it seemed that all roads led back there. It bore the scars of a city that had been bombed within an inch of its life less than twenty years before and had risen defiantly from the ruins and dereliction of the bombsites that still pockmarked its landscape.

This confidence was characterised – or, perhaps, articulated – in the explosion of experimental arts. Not only did Merseybeat encourage anyone with two hands to learn three chords on the guitar, but also poets performed, painters did their stuff and music was everywhere. The Liverpool Philharmonic Orchestra brought in hundreds of schoolchildren every year to explain and introduce them to the glorious possibilities of live classical music. Having peashooters fired at the cellos during Benjamin Britten's *Young Person's Guide to the Orchestra* seemed to annoy them, but never to deter them from persevering with their noble task. As a child I was already becoming familiar with Roger McGough, Brian Patten and the Mersey Poets. The Beatles led the way in popular music, but others accompanied them on their way. Comedians seemed to sprout up from nowhere and lend to the city the burden that still persists – that if you come from Liverpool you must be funny. And I haven't even started on the football yet.

Growing up in this place was deeply formative. It embedded in me all sorts of possibilities as well as prejudices. Growing towards adulthood in the 1970s was, for me at least, not easy. Pride in the place was tempered by the political battles on the City Council as people with diverse visions and motivations fought for the power to help this once-glorious city overcome its problems in order to forge a new and confident future. In school we were taught about the history of Liverpool and that its wealth was based on the profits of the transatlantic slave trade. Even going shopping with my parents into the city centre became a 'questioning' experience: the huge, solid, decorated and stately buildings that filled the city had been built with the blood of people who had been sold by their own people into slavery. As the rest of Great Britain seemed to be prospering in the 1970s and 1980s, Liverpool seemed to find it hard to escape its physical decline. Growing up with an enquiring mind and an emotional sensitivity was not comfortable and I think I always struggled to know how to express the conflicts within me.

Perhaps the city's status was best described by the slogan used by the Post Office on franked envelopes: 'Liverpool, city of change and challenge.' These words sat alongside an image of the new Post Office Tower with its revolving restaurant overlooking the resilient metropolis at its feet. The world was changing and the challenges were becoming serious. Optimism in the arts was not always reflected in the political or economic strategies of those elected to manage the change and help the people to face the challenges. I lived in a suburb of Liverpool, but saw the destruction of city-centre communities and the dispersal of people into newly built out-of-town estates. The social problems caused by these estates (high unemployment, poverty, vandalism, alienation) blighted the lives and prospects of several generations. Politicians seemed unaware of the effects that their political arguments and power plays had on these generations of ordinary people. Many of the estates I watched being built then have since been demolished. What has happened to the people who were subject to the great experiment I have no idea.

I am not seeking to justify or defend this perception of life as I grew up in Liverpool in the 1960s and 1970s. It is just how it was and how I remember it. Of course, my memories have also been shaped by people such as Mr Burrows, the sensitive English teacher who showed us John Lennon's 'doodle' book from his previous school, Quarry Bank. Another English teacher, Joan Talbot, inspired me with her enthusiasm for words and literature, opening up the possibility that not only special people could communicate in writing. Peter O'Connor, another English teacher, refused to let us get away with sloppy thinking and encouraged us not to think that only 'contemporary culture' had value, but that no culture meant anything unless one understood where it had come from. Denis Crighton, a German teacher, challenged my worldview and even introduced me to Dante. Probably none of these people knows the influence they had on me – and still have because they shaped the way I think and see the world.

The soundtrack to all this childhood and adolescent development was provided by the Beatles. The excitement every time a new single came out was palpable among people of all ages. These four lads transcended the boundaries of being stuck and opened up a whole new world of possibilities. I guess most of us dreamed at some point of being a pop star – at least, when we weren't dreaming of being a centre-forward for Liverpool Football Club. And the songs just kept on coming: dozens of them. They gave voice to the experiences and longings of a generation of young people. The protests of Bob Dylan and Joan Baez can also be found in Lennon and McCartney, but they never seem so angry or pointed. And it is songs about love and affection that still seem to characterise the prolific output of these great songwriters. Is it any wonder, for example, that *Yesterday* is the most covered song in the world, expressing as it does the longing and regret of a love that causes such agonising and turmoil?

But *Love Me Do* could be sung by anyone. *She Loves You* could be screamed by anyone who could bear to drop the Queen's English and yell 'yeah' several times. *Paperback Writer* puts into words what many readers of novels will have secretly thought. But then there are several songs that, although capable of a 'claim' by anyone anywhere anytime, have a special significance for those of us who identify with a particular place at the time it was written. Although I used to play football with my friends on the park at the back of *Strawberry Fields*, it is *Penny Lane* that brings me home.

The barber, showing photographs has long gone, but the shop is still a hairdresser's salon. As a teenager I went to Harry Bioletti's (as it was then) to get my hair cut. The banker – with his motorcar – is probably dead and buried by now, but the bank is still there to be seen – just opposite the shelter which is on the roundabout where the nurse was selling poppies. It is real. It is all there. I used to listen to the song and look at the places and wonder that the whole world could now sing about such an ordinary place that was just down the road from where I lived. It seemed oddly surreal. In one sense it was nothing to do with me, but I couldn't help feeling proud of it and identified with the song. Other people could sing it, but only Liverpool people could 'own' it.

Penny Lane is still there. The shelter on the round-about is there for a little longer, but it isn't looking healthy. My youngest son went to Liverpool University and was amazed to find himself living in halls of residence at the far end of Penny Lane from where Lennon and McCartney turned the ordinary into the special only a few decades before. (My elder son and his wife live not far from there.)

You can't be Nowhere

I have a vague memory of a British comedy character responding to an enquiry about his whereabouts (why he was where he was) by observing that everybody has got to be somewhere. And it is true. To be a human being means to be a body, to be physical and, therefore, living in a material world. There is no such thing as a disembodied person, but nor can there be a dislocated person. What I mean by this is that every human being lives somewhere, grows up somewhere, loves somewhere, dies somewhere. This might sound obvious, but it clearly is not obvious to people who think you can abstract people into categories and view them in a monolithic way as if they are all the same regardless of where they are. We are all shaped by where we were born and grew up, who our parents and carers were, what sort of school we went to, who our friends were and how we were taught or encouraged to see the world. The physical environment in which we grew up had some bearing on how we faced questions of individual and social meaning or significance. We did not grow up in a vacuum and we did not start out with a completely blank sheet.

Let me illustrate this (again) from my own experience. My parents belonged to a large Baptist church in Anfield, Liverpool. It was four or five miles from where we lived and until I was at primary school we didn't have a car. Friends used to transport us to and from church each Sunday and, as the years went by, during the week, too. The church was thriving and I remember there being huge numbers of children in the Sunday School. The horizons of my expectations involved moving on each September into the next class up and one day being big enough to join the youth group. I was keen to conform and enjoyed the approval that came from being 'good' at the church stuff. I remember being asked if I had 'asked Jesus into my heart' and saying 'yes' simply because I knew it was the right answer and that my problem with the literalness of the question was probably down to me being 'a bit thick'. Metaphysics wasn't the most strongly developed element of my intellectual life.

But this church did not only provide me with a strong community and a structure for weekly life, it also opened me to questions of human meaning, the reality of God, the identity of the Church and a particular understanding of right and wrong. It seems to me on reflection, however, that questioning these things was legitimate only within certain boundaries. Angst-ridden teenage Bible studies on 'sex', for example, were seen as a bold attempt to help us 'be Biblical'; but I look back on them as a tortuous struggle to tow the line. I wonder if I was the only one torn between the experience of being a growing human being and the strictures of a theology that saw sexual expression as inevitably sinful and deeply embarrassing even to God. Whatever the reality – and I do not doubt one iota the integrity of those attempting to live holy lives and help me to do the same – the result was an adolescence shaped by guilt and a fear of the consequences of disobeying God. This is ironic given that the dominant theology of the church there was that we are 'saved by grace' and cannot by our actions earn the love or approval of God. How, then, was I supposed to cope with the embarrassment of knowing what was happening inside my head and my body while knowing that God could see it all and probably hated me for it – especially as he didn't answer my prayers for him to deliver me from the internal conflict.

(I recall hearing many years later a man whose experience was similar to mine. He had been taught always to face any difficult ethical or behavioural dilemma with the question: 'What would Jesus do?' He had been encouraged to imagine Jesus standing in front of him, wherever he might be at the time. He said he didn't go to the toilet for a month.)

Yet this can be described in other ways, too. I grew up watching the physical redevelopment of Liverpool and seeing the struggles of many families to survive. I recognise that my reflections later in life might be selective and partial, but the memories I have are, quite simply, the memories I have. Liverpool was a place of high unemployment and alienation from a country that was being told it 'had never had it so good'. The physical dereliction of some parts of the built environment made a big impression on me. As a teenager I would get buses across town to get to Anfield and remember being constantly afraid of the skinheads, the dark places and the bus stops next to unprotected and badly lit bombsites. Whereas many people just transcended this sort of experience – or just ignored it and got on with their own life – I began to wonder how the contours of our experience of the environment in which we spend our formative years must shape our views of God, the world, self-value and relationships.

To put it more bluntly: if you grow up with dereliction, is it any surprise that you might begin to see the world through 'derelict' eyes?

Yet, 2008 saw Liverpool proudly celebrating its status as European City of Culture. This award recognised the achievement of a growing local economy, renewed self-confidence, restored pride and a thriving arts scene. The city has much to celebrate and its environment is showing once again evidence of a constructive view of the future. And even though I've been thirty years away from the city, its identity still courses through my veins.

The point of this excursion round the place of my birth and childhood is not, however, to paint a romantic picture or to cast aspersions on the motives or competence of those who were responsible for the life of the city during the tough 1960s to 1990s. It is simply a way of illustrating from personal experience how growing up in a particular place shapes a person for ever. My early life consisted of family, school and church – a particular family, a particular school and a particular church in a particular place in England at a particular time in history. My political convictions and prejudices were forged in a place where the privileges that appeared to be abundant in the south of England

11

were not to be found in the industrial north-west. Having spent seven years at a large comprehensive school in Liverpool, I found it difficult to cope with the affluence and confidence of public school children in Cheltenham when I eventually moved there in 1980. Again, I am not arguing here that one system is 'right' and another 'wrong'; I am simply illustrating that experience shapes worldview and that such prejudices (which are emotional as well as intellectual) are hard to shake off.

Childhood

Everybody has to be somewhere – and that 'somewhere' is a major factor in shaping who a person might become. But as soon as we begin to open this up we find other factors that matter enormously. It is well-known that the Jesuits used to say: 'Give me a boy until he is seven and I will give you the man.' Child psychologists are clear that the first four or five years of a child's life are deeply formative and, probably, the most important period for that child's future growth and development. For a child not to be loved, to be used or abused, to be neglected and not nurtured in body, mind and spirit, during those earliest years is not inconsequential.

Before he became Archbishop of Canterbury (leader of the Church of England and the worldwide Anglican Communion), Dr Rowan Williams addressed these matters in a challenging book called *Lost Icons* (T&T Clark, Edinburgh 2000). It is challenging not only because of the density of the writing, but because he asks questions that are not easy to face in a culture that is essentially pragmatic – concerned with what 'works' rather than what is 'true' – and uncomfortable with deeper questions of meaning (at least, when it comes to discussing it intelligently in public). In the introduction to the book he questions our confidence in what is meant by 'childhood' in contemporary culture and goes on to observe that the lack of such confidence destroys any coherent understanding of education. He develops these ruminations later in exploring what it means to speak of 'self' or 'soul' in a human being. But the theme that caught the imagination of many commentators – a theme that the Archbishop has returned to many times – was that of 'childhood' and his contention that somehow we have lost what it means to 'be a child' in contemporary Britain and beyond.

Williams's central idea might be summarised like this: we have lost the rituals that designated childhood and set it apart from adolescence and adulthood, and have turned children into consumers ('economic subjects') or 'pseudo-adults'. He argues that children are increasingly viewed as economic agents before they have been able to develop the faculties to cope with what being such an agent involves – counting the cost of risk, for example. Alongside the economic, he says, children are subjected to the advertising of 'desirability' and become 'sexual' agents. The nature of 'play' has changed and children are no longer being given the space to 'be' children. Williams suspects that this situation is partly attributable to a selfish adult culture in which children are unconsciously seen as rivals. He concludes that adults, by being childish themselves, prevent children from being allowed to be children. Instead, adults compete with children on the same behavioural stage. The book merits careful reading even though it is not an easy read. My purpose in citing it here is that

13

Williams raises questions that are uncomfortable and demand more urgent and serious attention.

Children are precious human beings and should not be seen as mere economic subjects or targets of advertisers' seductions. Experience shows that children reflect the values and models they have grown up with – that they are shaped unconsciously by what they experience of love and nurture and their opposites. A child will be shaped forever by the early experiences of life and relationships, and will not always understand why he sees the world in a particular way, why she either celebrates or fears close emotional engagement, why unconscious models of what it means to be (for example) a 'husband' or 'mother' seem so deeply ingrained.

And there are wider effects of our changed culture of childhood. The appalling abuse of young children for the gratification of adults should always shock a civilised and sensitised society of moral adults. But the response to this has been the creation of a culture of suspicion in which every adult is considered suspect until proven otherwise (in Britain) by Criminal Records Bureau checks (a theme developed by Dame Onora O'Neill in her 2002 Reith Lectures). It seems as if there has been a subtle shift from 'everyone should be trusted until proved otherwise' to 'nobody can be trusted until proved otherwise'. And, cutting a long argument short, we can only wonder what this element of our contemporary children's worldview in the UK will do to them as they shape the world for their own children's future. The cost might be worth paying in order to protect the few children who would otherwise suffer, but the wider cultural costs also need to be acknowledged.

The spiritual development and well-being of children is at least as important as their physical and psychological growth. Children display an ease of expression when it comes to asking 'why' questions, being generally or specifically curious, and even in relating to God. The social inhibitions have to be learned later, but children often express their 'faith' very openly and transparently. When Jesus put a child in the midst of his friends and told them they would have to become like this child if they were to enter the kingdom of heaven, clearly he had in mind precisely this sort of wondering curiosity and ability to trust – even where such vulnerability might eventually be confounded.

Being human

But why does any of this matter? Is it simply the sort of introspective reflection on a romanticised past age that marks the transition into middle age? Well, that may have a germ of truth in it. As one gets older and sees one's own children making their way in the world, it is impossible not to reflect on the successes and failings of parenthood. I cannot avoid tracing the patterns of nurture and discipline that I experienced as a child of my parents and detecting where they have been unwittingly replicated in the care of my own children. I find myself looking for those elements of continuity and discontinuity – where I have consciously decided to do things differently. But this reflective exercise cannot change the history, the actuality of the experience. Indeed, one of the humbling acknowledgements of parenthood is recognising that the history cannot now be re-written – the hope that our own children will not repeat the mistakes we made with them, and might even find better ways of parenting than we were able to exercise. Bringing up children is an imprecise art.

However, there is something much deeper than physical environment, parental models, social boundaries and economic value that shapes who we are and how we are. It is the fundamental understanding (assumptions?) we bring to what it means to be human in the first place. If I have a pragmatic understanding of 'being human' – one that suggests that there is no ultimate value or meaning other than what I choose to give it – it might well follow that economic value is the highest that can be attributed to someone. If life is a meaningless and random occurrence in which only the fittest survive the longest, it should come as no surprise if my pursuit of personal fulfilment appears to be the ultimate 'good'. Read any glossy magazine covers and these appear to be the ultimate measures of human worth: youth, beauty, success and satisfaction of 'need'.

It should not come as a surprise that this culture is essentially empty. We all grow old, lose our beauty, have our failings and learn that not every 'need' can be fulfilled. Nelson Rockefeller famously was asked how much was needed to make a man happy: 'just a little bit more' was his reply. Wealth might cushion us from many of the pains of life, but it cannot address the middle-of-the-night existential angst that questions why you ultimately matter. Strip everything else away and what are you left with – who are you?

Yet these are the sorts of question that human beings cannot avoid for ever. What we think about fundamental human value will shape how we bring up our children and how we choose to live together in human community. Our basic assumptions about human meaning will – whether we like it or not – have a direct influence on our behaviours and our ways of living, spending, giving, choosing, speaking, voting, and so on. So, it is surprising how rare it is to find people who have thought about why they assume what they do about human living and dying. At least, it is rare to find people who live consistently with the implications of the worldview they claim to assume.

These were questions that bugged me when I was growing up in the environment I described earlier in this chapter. When I was just starting secondary school at the age of 11 I found it hard to bring together the two worlds I inhabited: church and school. I felt a bit isolated in taking Jesus seriously and trying to understand the world with God in the frame. I read the Bible and tried to understand it without really realising there might be more than one way of reading it as a group of texts. I wanted to engage intellectually with it, but was happy to be given the 'answers' to the questions I sometimes articulated. I was a serious juvenile defender of 'creationism' before I understood the term and I ridiculed theories of evolution as being 'wrong because unbiblical'. When we sang hymns in school assembly at the beginning of the day I was the only one to sing – which is not funny when you are 14, your voice has broken and everyone else is laughing at you. I did it simply because I had a firm conviction that I could not let myself be shaped by the pressure of the crowd – even if it was a relatively trivial matter such as singing a hymn, I would not allow myself to be cowed into silence just in order to conform.

I look back on those days now with a mixture of embarrassment and pride: embarrassment at how difficult I must have been for my friends and teachers, but pride that I learned not to be afraid to be ridiculed for what I believed to be true. And this is where the threads of this chapter begin to come together. However naïve some of my understandings of God, the world and people might have been, at least I grew up being encouraged to think about what really mattered in life, and being challenged to make decisions and life-choices in the light of something deeper than consumerism or acquisition of 'stuff' and things. It could be said that I grew up thinking through what it means to be human, why it matters and what the implications of my convictions might be for everybody else.

The 'Image of God'

The conclusion I came to – having struggled with the Bible, talked with people and wrestled with my own inner thoughts and desires – was that being human has to be rooted in something or someone beyond the particular human person that is 'me' today. If the only meaning I have is the meaning I choose to give to my life, then the consequences for myself and others are not necessarily pleasant. If my goal is to fulfil myself, I might have to ensure that others who stand in my way will not fulfil themselves – after all, whose right to fulfilment has priority? What, then, would I say to the charge that 'you don't ultimately matter'? Well, I would respond with the simple and mysteriously profound statement that has motivated millions of people during the centuries to lives of love, sacrifice and service: I am made in the image of God – and that is why I ultimately matter, even if the whole world says I do not.

In Genesis 1 the poet has God creating human beings 'in his own image' and setting them free to cultivate the earth. They are free from inhibition or fear of the Creator or each other. If they 'reflect' the Creator, then they are to be creative, free, liberating and loving. They have the power to choose and to refrain from choosing. But, ultimately, it means that each person is unique, valuable, irreplaceable and infinitely loved. This, it seems to me, is where the value of the anonymous child lying on a pile of bodies in Auschwitz is to be found: discarded by the world, but eternally loved by the God who shaped him in his mother's womb. Human beings have meaning and ultimate importance not because they simply choose so, but because of their origin as created beings.

This is what moved the writer of Psalm 139 to struggle with the mystery of having been 'knit together in my mother's womb' (v. 8), but not hidden from the loving gaze of the God who is also far greater than all we can imagine. To be created means to live in time and space as a mortal being whose choices and decisions ultimately matter. Our children – and how we raise them to see themselves and address these deep questions of self-value – are not simply buckets of emptiness to be filled by whatever dominates the particular cultural world of their day; rather, they are persons, created and contingent, mortal and eternal, moral and accountable – but they are children who need the space to grow and learn and emulate and rebel and make their own way in the world, conscious of who they are and why they ultimately matter. Only thus can they shape their children's world in a way that allows all people to know 'who they are' and 'why they matter'.

My upbringing has shaped me and contributed to who I am today. That will inevitably have elements that are good, but it will also have elements that are regrettable. But the particularity of my being born in Liverpool in November 1957, growing up in my family, going through my schools with my teachers, and wrestling with questions of 'meaning' within my particular context have all added to the mix that has resulted in me being who I am today. Penny Lane is still there and the memories will never fade, but I moved on into a bigger world – even though I can never fully leave behind those factors which formed me out of the early years of my experience. Childhood and its environment matters enormously, as do the questions we must ask about what vision of humanity it is that fires our understanding and directs our choices in making our particular world what it is ... and what it might become.

Chapter 2

IMAGINE

One of the great questions (for me, at least) of the 1980s and early 1990s was: will the Beatles ever get back together? If so, how? The rift between John Lennon and Paul McCartney was deep enough to have been exposed in some mutually bitter songs, but all four of the Beatles seemed to have gone their own ways. It seems doubtful that they would have sought to boost their pensions in the way so many bands have done in the first decade of the twenty-first century. Anyway, the question was resolved unequivocally and brutally with the slaughter of John Lennon in the stairwell to his apartment block in New York on 8 December 1980.

As I was growing up in Liverpool I developed a great admiration for John Lennon in particular. He seemed to have that streak of bloody-minded obstinacy that at the same time is both admirable and irritating. He stuck his finger up to authority and hierarchies, made grand gestures and questioned everything. He exemplified the two sides of the caricatured northern Englishman: he spoke plainly, regardless of how it might be heard or received, but was then easily hurt when anyone did the same back to him. The hard, questioning, angry exterior was clearly protective of an internal vulnerability and humanity that found its way out in great music.

So, how did someone as thoughtful, passionate and complex come to write something as stupid as *Imagine*? In poll after poll towards the turn of the millennium this song came out as the most popular song of all time (whatever that means). Maybe it is because it presses all the right sentimental buttons in people who just wish the world could be different and better – usually without costing them anything to bring the change about. But, whatever the reasons – both rational and emotional – it remains a silly song and I am mystified how Lennon could have written it. I will return to this later.

But, for now, let's stick with Lennon the person. I once wrote a radio script for BBC radio about 'mole men'. Moles, I explained, ruined our garden in Leicestershire by burrowing under the lovely lawn and emerging in unexpected places, making a huge disruptive mess as they did. They could not be stopped from digging beneath the surface and spoiling the calm beauty of superficial appearance. It seemed to me that some people are like this: they are never satisfied with superficiality or blandness, especially where these are designed to preserve illusions of satisfaction or complacency with the status quo. They keep asking 'why?' and not being satisfied with attempts to duck the crucial issue. Such people are a nightmare in the pub. I cited Jesus as a 'mole man' – one who wouldn't let people get away with their political games in which other people became mere pawns for the purpose of proving someone else's argument. He placed question marks over the fundamentals of religious belief and power, leaving his interlocutors to take responsibility for the conclusions they either drew or avoided. And, while being careful not to give rise to a headline that suggests 'Bishop says John Lennon is God', I think John Lennon was a bit like Jesus in this particular respect (if in no other).

Lennon had the irritating habit of putting into words what other people were trying either to articulate or silence. Whether it was asking Paul McCartney 'how do you sleep at night?' or challenging the 'powers-that-be' with a peace protest that involved staying in bed for a long time, he made his frustrations clear. The seminal 1970 New York interview he did with Jann Wenner for *Rolling Stone* magazine is almost painful to listen to: passionate, angry, bitter, sarcastic, eloquent – it was Lennon at his most sharp and acerbic. But it also showed how wounded he was at the rejection of Yoko Ono by the other Beatles. In some of his songs he wore some of these barely suppressed emotions on his sleeve and made no attempt to hide from the consequences.

But he was also a massive hypocrite of breathtaking proportions and it is for this that I think he should be applauded. He never pretended to be consistent or pure or to have every circle squared. The fact that he was an immensely rich man living in a world of unimaginable privilege did not deter him from writing such nonsense as *Imagine*. His own personal hypocrisy and inconsistency was not something he felt the need to defend, but neither could it silence him from expressing his anger at the world's apparent injustices and imbecility. In other words, he was not narcissistic enough to keep quiet in case anyone spotted the gaps between his protestations and his lifestyle.

So, why do I say that *Imagine* is stupid? Well, it is basically because it is more about fantasy than imagination. Whereas it might be possible to imagine that there is no heaven, there is something a bit odd (at the very least) about a bloke singing of a happy world without possessions while sitting at a grand piano in a flashy apartment in the financial capital of a country that equates its fundamental raison d'être (God's endorsement of the 'land of the free') with the acquisition of wealth and things. 'Imagine no possessions apart from the ones I've got and don't want to give up' might have been more accurate, but clearly would not have fitted the tune.

Nevertheless, despite all this, there is still something good to be found among the nonsense in this song. For it calls people to go beyond the tangible and visible, the immediate and the status quo, and to 'imagine' a different world, a different way of being and living and relating to people, the world and things. It is now something of a cliché that students in Europe and America in the 1960s and 1970s were so idealistic and committed to transforming the world that they would campaign, protest and sit-in in order to bring about change. Dissatisfaction with the way power was wielded and values assumed – and motivated (sometimes consciously) by Karl Marx's injunction that the point of politics is not to talk about a different world but to change the one we are in and create a new one that is different – moved young people to act.

Yet those days seem a long way away. Maybe it is fear of the future or simply the fact of debt, but it is indisputable that the heady days of idealism and activism are long gone. One UK university professor summed up contemporary student conviction as: 'give me the quote to put in the essay to get me the marks to get me the degree that will get me the job I need to get me the money to get me the things that will make my life complete.' If he is right, then we are witnesses to a tragedy. Over 2,500 years ago a poet suggested that where young people have no vision, they have no future.

The idealism and activism of the 1960s and 1970s might well have been naïve and sometimes narcissistic, but it at least challenged the status quo and imagined a better world. Granted, it was a world with fewer technological distractions and fewer entertainment possibilities. But it was a world in which many young people in Europe questioned the fundamental values of and explanations for the world in which we live. We were not anaesthetised by 'stuff' or by beginning adult life with such huge debts that our future was seen in resolving or negotiating our way through some financial minefield. Pragmatism did not rule and there was some inkling that the world could be run differently and could be re-ordered in a more humane way. The personal commitment of the sit-in appears to have given way to maybe signing up for a £5 monthly direct debit in favour of an animal charity. Even in the light of the huge financial debts with which students begin their adult life in Britain today, it still seems very anaemic.

Yet, what John Lennon grasped is that imagination is fundamental to who we are as human beings. What distinguishes us from other animals is our ability to imagine something beyond ourselves and our current 'reality' and to work to create it. We write, tell stories, play with what we have (material) in order to open our minds and hearts to different ways of seeing (art and music). Our fear of the future – or for what the future might or might not hold – is tamed by an imagination that opens up different possibilities. Imagination is essential to wonder, and wonder is what makes a difference to human experience – taking us beyond what we currently think we know and experience and allowing us to dream and yearn and hope.

Wonder

Children seem to be born with an openness to possibilities that are both real and unreal. They begin to shape the world they live in by playing with words, images, stories and ideas in ways that will eventually lead to an ability to distinguish between what is real and what is imagined. They are able to live with not having rationally to analyse a fairy story or deconstruct a cartoon character. A child can live with and within an expansive world in which she doesn't have to be limited by the immediate. However, an education system that sees children as potential economic producers and consumers is not likely to give value to what is not quantifiable on someone's eventual balance sheet. If a child is simply and cynically seen as a 'figure' to be courted in order to encourage a lifelong allegiance to a particular bank, style or brand, then he has been either deliberately or blindly dehumanised. At least, this is true if you believe that human beings are more than the sum of their economic potential. Education should surely be about developing human beings as people who can contribute to the humanising of all people everywhere, starting in their own family and community.

Imagination is rooted in the capacity to wonder and exercised in the pursuit of curiosity. A child grows up small in a limited world constituted by its family and immediate physical environment. As the child grows this world expands and becomes more complicated. But the experience of seeing it expand marries with the inherent capacity to play and dream and stretch reality in ways that are fun, expressive of a desire for escape (or for a different reality) or just fantastical. The child knows that people neither live forever nor can fly out of windows; but it doesn't stop Peter Pan being 'real' or hinder the longing for a Tinkerbell to bring some magic to ordinary life, helping us to transcend the parts of our experience or environment that limit us or cause us pain. Of course, Captain Hook is capable of bearing many different faces that give form and shape to fear or threat.

But children can also wonder at things beyond themselves without having to articulate the experience or reduce it to the manageable shape of mere words. Why should a child have to describe a sunset if he can paint it? In a famous *Peanuts* cartoon, Charlie Brown is sitting with Snoopy the dog on the edge of what looks like a cliff, looking up at the starry universe above them. And he simply wonders about the smallness of himself and his life in the context of the vastness and 'eternity' of the universe. Notably, he just lives with the overwhelming and mysterious 'bigness' of it all and doesn't need to articulate it for the sake of rationalists. The Old Testament poet, on the other hand, responds to the same experience as an adult and asks: 'When I look at your heavens, the work of your fingers, the moon and the stars that you have established; what are human beings that you are mindful of them, mortals that you care for them?' (Psalm 8:3–4). All human beings are capable of wonder and expressing it in different ways; what worries me is the children who have that capacity drained from them by early experiences of life and people who scorn imagination, regard 'wonder' as a romantic luxury and reinforce the assumption that 'this is all there is'.

I have yet to hear any serious commentator explore the 'loss of wonder' when describing or analysing the gang cultures of modern cities such as London or New York. What happens to children and teenagers whose experience of life and the world is such that their horizons are reduced to the acquisition of status objects (icons of belonging) or mere personal physical survival (knife culture)? What has happened to their mind's freedom to wonder and wander and be curious about the world and its significance? Where is their capacity to imagine or their freedom to be motivated by curiosity rather than by fear? What is it about our culture that assumes that everybody is to be suspected and nobody is to be trusted – that life is both to be risk-free and yet at the same time totally threatening?

Worldviews

Living and working in London means that one is confronted daily by diverse communities of people who face significant challenges – challenges not only in respect of negotiating an overcrowded transport system or finding the best schools for their children. A paramount challenge is to discern what are the most powerful factors that shape the worldview of those who live there, especially the children and young people. A worldview can be defined as the 'lens behind the eyes through which we see God, the world and ourselves' and conclude without critical reflection that 'that is just the way the world is'. In other words, every human being has a view of the world *for which* they rarely argue and which they merely *assume*. Unfortunately, this lens is rarely taken out and examined in order to see whether or not it is realistic.

The point about worldviews is that they are shaped by a number of factors including childhood experience, parental influence, friendships, education and nurture. But they are also shaped by the built environment, assumptions about society and other people, good and bad relationships, mass media (including ubiquitous music and advertising), the internet and television. Visual images and aural assaults create and shape the lens through which, for example, teenage boys think of girls and their sexuality: are girls sexual objects to be 'won' or exploited, or are they people with whom mutual relationships can be grown to mutual benefit? Is violence the only way to ensure personal safety or establish identity in the crowd? And is there more to life than what seems to be presented to me on the estate in which I live? It is clear that we now have a generation of young people whose answers to these questions will not encourage the rest of us.

I guess it comes down to a pretty fundamental question: is this all there is? Children who grow up to believe that there is nothing beyond what is tangible, visible or palatable can be forgiven for assuming that the most valuable goal in life is merely to survive for as long as possible. But this is very worrying and I want to explore briefly why, referring back to John Lennon's *Imagine*.

Imagine No Religion ...

Lennon invites us to imagine a world in which there is no religion and the 'bait' of heaven is rejected. Echoing the Marxist critique of religion being the 'opiate of the people', seducing or threatening them to conform with the status quo of contemporary exploitative power relationships in order to guarantee 'heaven' after death, Lennon sees 'religion' as a negative force used by negative people to subjugate or infantilise people who otherwise might be released to live for themselves. He sees religion as a fantasy that people should grow out of, then finding themselves in the 'adult' world of freedom and dignity. But, in doing so, Lennon ignores a fact that many contemporary commentators also seem to find difficulty in admitting: Lennon's own worldview is not neutral and the world he commends (freed from the scourge of religion) is not neutral either. He seems to assume that if only we could excise religion from human society everything would be all right, conflict would end and people would live in harmony with each other.

Now, this might fit within the remit of a pop song with a good tune, but it is pathetic when subject to a few seconds rational critique by a 5-year-old child. The secular humanist (if that is a reasonable way to describe John Lennon) assumes that his own worldview is neutral and that religious people hold a 'loaded' worldview that is, therefore, dangerous. The commitment religious people apply to the object of their worship or worldview is to be suspected because it refuses to deny implications and consequences for all other worldviews. Lennon lets the cat out of the bag in this song when he merely assumes that his own worldview is neutral, not loaded, is somehow 'natural' and self-evidently true. Yet it is precisely this arrogance that he condemns in religious people.

Any worldview is based on and shaped by assumptions about life, meaning and value; it can never be neutral or purely rationally negotiated. Richard Dawkins might object to the fact, but even his way of seeing and thinking is 'loaded' and 'committed' by assumptions he brings to the way he lives his life and gives value to people, relationships and things. And yet, what does the Lennon worldview offer us – apart from a not-very-thought-through snarl at religion (as if 'religion' was a monolithic phenomenon)? I would argue it offers us a bland and overly optimistic view of the world in which we just have to hope that human beings might turn out to be basically lovely and will allow everyone to do their own thing as and when and how they like. It is a fantasy of epic proportions to think that human beings are governed by their rational faculties alone and can somehow 'mature' morally into something benign without a single shred of evidence from history that this is even remotely realistic. The Soviet model (of atheistic humanism – or inhumanism – that cost millions of innocent lives) was not notably successful in this respect.

Yet this nonsense is reflected every day in our so-called 'mature' society. A whole generation of teachers has been trained in the United Kingdom with the assumptions that (a) religion is not neutral (and therefore dangerous), (b) that all religions are basically the same, but allow for peculiarities of diet and fashion, and (c) that their critically unexamined secular humanism *is* neutral and self-evidently true.

When an Islamist group attempted to car-bomb Glasgow Airport in 2007 the local police called in all leaders of faith communities in my area for an emergency meeting. I was unable to attend at such short notice, but phoned to ask what was the purpose and hoped-for outcome of the meeting. I was told that it was vital to reduce tension between religious groups in order to avoid conflict. I replied that there was no evidence that there had been, was now or would be in the future any conflict between faith communities in this area. Rather, the problem was with the disaffected racist un(der)employed white youth who were never to be found in a worship centre for any religion. But this uncritical prejudice saw the people with religious conviction as being potentially more problematic than those who are 'irreligious'.

Now, that raises a further interesting matter. There are those in contemporary society who hold no religious convictions or beliefs and who claim to be 'without faith' or 'non-believing'. On the face of it, this looks to be a perfectly reasonable position to hold and the epithets seem unproblematic. But 'without faith' or 'non-believing' can only be applied to such people if you actually believe that it is possible to live an entirely rational life and believe nothing about the world, morality, history, life, etc. Everyone believes something about the world for which they do not argue and which they merely assume: that life can be meaningful, for example; or that relationships matter; or that it is 'wrong' (as opposed to 'merely inconvenient') to kill someone. The list of examples could go on, but the point seems so obvious and should not need spelling out at all. Every human being believes certain things about why the world is the way it is and puts their faith into the world actually being that way. No human being has no faith and no human being believes in nothing. This is not just a bit of linguistic pedantry – it matters that the fantasy of the secular humanist worldview is exposed for what it is and that people who use such language should be challenged to use their 'rationality' consistently.

Worship

So, where does all this lead us? Well, firstly it brings us to a point where we can acknowledge the nonsensical unreality of John Lennon's totalitarian dream. Imagine there is 'no heaven' if you will, but you can't run away from asking why you think that 'earth' matters at all in any objectively recognisable way. Imagine 'no religion' if you will, but don't think this lets you off the hook of justifying and living consistently within a world in which meaning and significance are merely assumed, 'rights' are claimed (without any justification other than that they *are*), morality is arbitrarily established and people like Richard Dawkins try to escape the critical intellectual challenge they impose on those who 'believe'.

Furthermore, this vision of a religionless world seems to call for a monochrome and cultureless society in which only those who believe in the 'here and now' and 'this and that' are to be tolerated or valued. And even furthermore still, it seems to assume that it is possible to believe things without there being any need to commit oneself to the consequences of what is believed. John Lennon never got as far as exploring the problems of the world he was calling for; he simply tried to call for the abolition of the bits of this world that he found personally inconvenient.

In 2003 I represented the Archbishop of Canterbury at a Congress of Leaders of National and Traditional Religions in Kazakhstan. The day before the congress itself began I was taken with a colleague to the media centre where I was informed I would be briefing the world's media on the ensuing interfaith dialogue. A fifteen-minute speech (which had not been requested beforehand) would be followed by forty minutes of engagement with the assembled media people and a five-minute live television interview. During the forty-minute press conference I was asked by a young, optimistic and enthusiastic Russian television journalist if I thought there would ever be a single world religion. The implication was that we would all agree on an unproblematic and anodyne set of beliefs which would enable the world to be at peace. I replied that I did not foresee any such world religion and that I thought that such a vision would be best described as 'totalitarian'. The use of this word did not appeal to my more diplomatic English colleague, but I remain sure that it was apposite. What would be the commitments that would characterise such a religion and how would such a religion be ordered (especially in its political, economic and social content and implications) in such a way as to guarantee its universality? Presumably, deviance would somehow have to be proscribed and the boundaries policed. And isn't such a vision 'totalitarian' in nature? The Russian journalist, recently escaped from the shackles of Soviet 'freedom' and yearning for a bright future, got the point immediately and understood that visions have to be critiqued and cashed out.

What, for example, would art look like in such a world? What vision and commitment would inspire musicians to lift the heart and reach places words and images cannot reach? In what would such art and music consist? If 'this' is all there is, then to what transcendent end would all this aspire?

But all of this brings us back to the point of what it means to be a human being who is capable of imagining something beyond what is immediately apparent in the physical world. Why do we dream dreams and imagine a different reality? What is it about human beings that makes us able to hope when the evidence of our experience seems to militate against such aspiration? And why is religious vision and commitment seen by some as fantasy when their own imagination is deemed beyond criticism or justification?

The Christian response to these questions is to insist that religious belief, commitment and experience need to be put out there in the public realm and allowed to be questioned. They can never be private, even if they are always personal. Christians will argue with a confident humility that the human ability to imagine is connected inextricably to our capacity to wonder, and that both are rooted in the nature of human beings as being created and constitutionally compelled to worship.

'Worship' is, simply put, the giving of value to what matters in life. Thomas Carlyle described worship as 'transcendent wonder'. In his Sonnet 106 William Shakespeare encapsulates the experience of worship that transcends mere words:

> For we, which now behold these present days,
> Have eyes to wonder, but lack tongues to praise.

In the case of the ordinary Christian, worship is rooted in the fact that we are made in the image of God and capable of holding within us a concept of the eternal – and this works its way out in the expression of worship in all its human diversity. In this sense, worship is not merely about telling God how great he is (he has probably worked it out for himself by now), but about growing in a relationship with the Creator in which the whole of life's experiences can be owned, exposed, welcomed, lamented, regretted and transcended. Worship, for the Christian, is the expression of freedom to be loved and, in response, to love the Creator. This liberates us to live responsively in the world now with trust in the Creator for whatever will follow.

As we saw earlier, the early Jewish writers and Psalmists gave expression to their experience of wonder at the enormity of the universe and the need to respond to the One who pours himself into it – leaving fingerprints of his activity and touch everywhere, if only we can see them. They make a connection between their experience of the 'numinous' and the need to respond to what is greater than themselves and their own particular experience. They recognise within the human person the image of the loving Creator who exists in relationship and beckons the imagination to reach out beyond what is merely or apparently evident.

One of the clearest examples of what this looks like is to be found in the writings of the Old Testament prophets. The people of Israel were taken into captivity in the eighth century BC and the sixth century BC. The foreign empires had invaded and sent many of the people and their leaders into exile. Given that Judaism assumes that God is not just a tribal deity, but is the Creator and sustainer of the entire universe, this turn of events is more than just embarrassing. Psalm 137 encapsulates the predicament in the most abject and anguished language, bemoaning the taunts of the captors who mock the exiles with calls to 'sing the songs of . . .' er . . . 'the *Lord* . . .' (hmmm!)' while you sit in defeat on the banks of the rivers of Babylon. The evidence of your circumstances and your experience tells you that the God in whom you trust is either weaker than the other tribal gods (or why else are you here?) or that he doesn't exist. Either way, your identity, worldview and history are questioned at their very roots by what has happened to you. Surely, to speak now of your faith in your God is mere fantasy?

Well, as Walter Brueggemann explains in several of his books on the Old Testament prophetic writings, the prophets were those who reminded the exiles of their story, their identity, their vocation and their language of home. They kept hope alive where to do so seemed stupidly pointless. Empires always look powerful and invincible, but history teaches us that they also always come and go. So, the prophets encourage the people to take a long-term view and to remember that 'this' is not all there is. It is probably in just this context that the Creation narratives of Genesis were written to remind people that the God in whom 'the beginning' came to be takes his time and will not ultimately be mocked: but God's people are called to be those who live now as if a different world existed. The prophets call for the people to hold onto the possibility of what might be called a new beginning after loss – that is, to keep alive the vision for their existence that is not denied even by the most excruciating of circumstances.

This is where imagination has to be rooted in something or someone trustworthy. Imagination enables us to wonder and wonder evokes worship (inevitably and in some form or other) and worship demands commitment with consequences.

Back to Lennon

So, even if I find myself loving John Lennon's *Imagine* but thinking its content is silly, I also applaud the fact that imagination is celebrated (even if not justified) by him. My concern, however, is for those who as children are brought up in circumstances in which the spirit of imagination is crushed and the possibility of 'newness after loss' seems like fantasy because the worldview of the dominant culture is so sterile. I fear for the children whose environment turns their eyes to the dust instead of lifting them to the skies in wonder. I am anxious for those young people whose lives have been characterised by a lack of beauty, a fear of the transcendent or a mocking of the spiritual. I regret a society that bombards us with values rooted in things and stuff and image and then wonders why some young people seem unable to see beyond themselves and their immediate circumstances.

I attended a large comprehensive school in Liverpool and was inspired by two English teachers and a German teacher. They saw beyond the over-serious and narrow-minded teenager and pushed me (perhaps without ever realising it) to want more, to explore more, and to trust that something is true because it is true and not because it is convenient (or 'Christian'). They got me to read beyond the curriculum and gave time to argue with me when I must have been a trial and a pain to them. But they encouraged me to push deeper, ask questions, not be afraid of what I might discover. They teased my imagination and fed my curiosity without ever patronising or judging me. And I owe them a huge debt for this great gift: they knew instinctively that education was not primarily about teaching, but about enabling people like me to learn.

It seems to me that the job of education is not to fill empty vessels with more stuff, but to awaken curiosity, stir the imagination and evoke the sort of wonder that will never be satisfied with the superficial. In Christian terms I would maintain that curiosity is the key to the kingdom of God – the sort of searching and questioning that refuses to be stultified by the simplistic, and probes until something more substantial is encountered. Jesus did not encourage his friends to follow him in order to be followers of Jesus, but in order that they might recognise the God who loves them and become more fully human by responding in love to him. It might never find expression in great songs or poems or paintings; but it will always lift the soul to contemplate the inarticulate wonder of the Creator behind the Creation that whispers incessantly of love and hope and generosity.

Chapter 3

LORD OF THE STARFIELDS

Music has played a big part in my life. At the age of 11 I was singing in school choirs and even sang a solo of 'Ye spotted snakes with double tongue' in a school production of Shakespeare's *A Midsummer Night's Dream*. Unfortunately, I remember that particular set of performances for two embarrassing reasons: first, I had to wear green tights and a girl's white blouse with puffy sleeves; second, my voice chose to begin to break on the first night. I progressed onto playing the trumpet and managed to be conducted on one occasion in a wind band in Liverpool by the 16-year-old Simon Rattle (now Sir Simon Rattle, Principal Conductor of the Berlin Philharmonic Orchestra). I played classical music with the school orchestra and eventually played with one of my sisters in the Liverpool Schools Orchestra – even performing in the world premier of a specially commissioned piece at St Paul's Cathedral in London.

At this time – during my teenage years – I tried hard to love classical music and scorned anything else. My elder brother's liking for Led Zeppelin, Deep Purple, Cream and others, simply incurred my incredulous suspicion. But then I joined a small jazz group and discovered the wonders of the blues, of Dixieland

and of contemporary swing. I loved listening to Louis Armstrong and upsetting the binmen by playing David Rose's *The Stripper* at high volume from my bedroom. Jazz – especially improvised jazz – intrigued me, even though I didn't always understand what was going on. The fact that there was a basic line or chord around which the members of the band played seemed risky and dangerous: after all, one of them might mess it up. But the risk was what gave the music its edge and its sense of pushing at the boundaries of what was safe. Indeed, it burst with life and fun while at the same time dealing lyrically with the stuff of real life and death. Jazz was often, if not usually, very rude and had its own codes for those who had the ears to understand. It told stories, had a laugh, mourned loss and celebrated life with verve, imagination and a total lack of pomposity.

The edginess of jazz and the seemingly reckless fun of those who played it were very attractive, but I was also the sort of teenager who wanted to be safe and to play life safely. I didn't want to get things wrong and was fearful of transgressing the rules of a judging God. Put into that mix all that goes into jazz and, later, rock music and you will understand the potent concoction of multiple angsts that seem in retrospect to have characterised my adolescence. I began to play my brother's guitar and quickly moved on to buying my first 'proper' guitar, a small-bodied Yamaha acoustic. This arose from an awakening to acoustic and rock music with my careful listening to Paul Simon, The Beatles, Yes, Focus, Pink Floyd and others. The first two records I ever bought were Black Sabbath's *Paranoid* and something by Kenny Ball and his Jazzmen: how's that for confusion? One of my all-time favourite records was by a group of session trumpeters in the United States, *Tutti's Trumpets*, but eventually the dog chewed it to the point where only two tracks remained playable. Somehow, the dog survived.

Over the years since then I have listened to anything and everything from world music through to modern jazz via rock, country and opera. The world is full of music and there simply isn't time to listen to it all. Every day new musicians emerge and I find they give voice and a vocabulary to things I think and feel and experience, but in words and sounds that I could never have found for myself. Worldviews are expressed or unveiled that make me reflect on my own. Music has the ability to get underneath the rational and reflective and subvert the emotions – those parts of being human that we think we have under control. But it can also open the soul to the vast expanse of what cannot be grasped or contained by the limitations of the human mind or consciousness. In other words, it can open us up to *wonder* (both as a noun and a verb).

A Dream Like Mine ...

I didn't discover Bruce Cockburn (http://en.wikipedia. org/wiki/Bruce_Cockburn) until the age of 27 when I was at Theological College in Bristol. A friend introduced me to his music and I have never since then been able to shake him off. Cockburn is a Canadian singer-songwriter with a limited-but-loyal following in the UK and is much better known in North America. Born in 1945 in Ottawa, by 2008 he had released twenty-nine albums ranging from eco-folk through rock, jazz and country to his own unique brand of conscience-searing and beautiful (but hard to define) ... er ... music. The albums chart his life experience and the development of his convictions and understandings of the world, relationships and God.

He ranges over the years from the deeply intimate to the global and universal, wrestling en route through cutting poetry and sublime guitar playing with politics, economics, culture and ecology. It is impossible to listen to *If I Had a Rocket Launcher* without feeling a raging anger toward the American powermongers who sanctioned the helicopter gunship attacks on villagers in Nicaragua who had made the unfortunate mistake of voting for the wrong government. You can feel the tension he is wrestling with as a pacifist when he decides that in these circumstances – sitting in a ditch in a village while the bullets rain down – that if he had the weapons to hand, he would blow the helicopter and its crew out of the sky.

Cockburn doesn't sanitise his songs in order to soften the blow for his more sensitive audience. He draws from his own sensibilities as he derides the trickle-down myths of free-market economics. He explores the contradictions of human relationships and the complexities of loving and being loved. Yet he also laughs at the inanity of a culture that wants a guarantee of total security in life and sues anyone who disturbs the myth: in *Anything can Happen*, he suggests it is probably wise not to get out of bed in the morning if you want a risk-free existence.

But Cockburn did something else for me. I have read endless poetry and read numerous books. I have read the Bible many times through and I have enjoyed art all over the world. I have marvelled at the capacity of new technology to reveal the vastness and minuscule tininess of the universe. I have scrutinised the first pictures of earth from the moon and stared for hours at the amazing images compiled by the Hubble telescope. But it was a simple song from Cockburn's early period that gave me the words to hang all this together and provide me with a vocabulary for connecting the bigness of the universe with the smallness of me in a language of worship: *Lord of the Starfields* takes hackneyed epithets for God the Creator and fires them with new power and meaning. The 'Ancient of Days' – the 'universe maker' – is praised and then, in the refrain, implored to inspire the singer with love.

What Cockburn does in this song is to evoke wonder. As noted in the last chapter, it is the experience we read about in Psalm 8:3–4 when, in a Charlie Brown moment of existential vulnerability, the poet says: 'When I consider your heavens, the work of your fingers, the moon and the stars, which you have set in place, what is [man] that you are mindful of him the son of man that you care for him?' Most of us live our lives in a frenetic whirl of activity and rarely find life's routines and pressures allowing us the space to stop and stare and wonder at the 'meaning' questions thrown up by contemplation of the universe and 'me'. Cockburn tries to imagine the creative mind of God whose 'dream' cannot be dulled or dismissed: if you share God's creative dream then nothing can drag you down. However, he recognises in his songs that most of us do not hang onto the dream and have become impervious to the playful creativity of the God who laughed creation into being. We are preoccupied with looking down at the ground and don't notice the vastness of the firmament above and around.

45

If, like me, you live in a huge urban environment, it is possible to go for years without really seeing the sky and its stars – the light pollution hangs a veil of dimness over us, thus hiding from us the sense of depth we see as we look into the light years of blackness 'out there'.

In April 2007 I took a group of twenty people from my Episcopal Area to visit our Link Diocese of Central Zimbabwe. We flew into Harare and then went by bus to Gweru where we stayed first at St Patrick's Mission up in the hills outside the town. When darkness fell it was truly dark. In fact, because of the power cut that hit just as the sun went down, it was totally dark ... apart from the moon and the stars. Each evening we were there a group of us took chairs outside where we sat on the grass and stared at the sky for a couple of hours. The depth of the vision was startling: millions of stars clustered and spread across the unfathomable heavens and it was impossible to avert our eyes from the intensity and complex beauty of the speckled canvas above us. Shooting stars came and went (as they do) – and everyone else saw them except me. I finally understood what Paul Simon means in the song *Under African Skies* on his *Graceland* album. Words fail and conversation can feel intrusive when you stare into the depths of the universe and contemplate the meaning or significance of your own little and transient life.

It is surely this capacity to wonder, to see and imagine beyond ourselves and the reality we experience, that makes us human and unique. So, why does that capacity appear to be so starved and the implications of wonder seem to be so feared in contemporary western culture? Maybe it is because the dominant cultures of the late twentieth and early twenty-first centuries have taught us that the only things that matter are those that can be measured. Education is not a 'good' in its own right, but must be seen to produce economic agents who can produce a measurable contribution to the economy. Politics can sometimes appear to be driven by economics – maybe even by particular economic dogmas – to the extent that the intended 'end' of politics ceases to be 'the common good' (in human, cultural or ecological terms) and becomes instead 'a growing economy making people feel good and thus bringing social stability'. But, as suggested in the last chapter, if our children are brought up with a worldview that unconsciously marks only the measurably successful as being valuable, it can be little wonder that the value of merely 'being' is implicitly derided. If a person is seen as a mere consumer, why should he or she see anyone else (let alone themselves) as intrinsically valuable or meaningful?

I grew up in an age when there was no daytime television and 'news' wasn't being broken upon us every minute of the day. There was space to play and time to get bored. School was important, but targets weren't driving education and the obsession with economic markers such as league tables had not yet darkened the scene. Maybe my memory is selective and romantic, but I seem to remember being encouraged to use my imagination, to explore the world, to learn to read because there was so much out there to be read and discovered. In other words, I didn't ever feel that I was being groomed to take my place as a cog in an economic wheel or that I would be valued for ever according to either my output or my accumulation of things. Maybe there was just the space to be and to play that children always enjoy – but we weren't driven to endless activities, given endless access to sound and visual stimulation or taken to 'extra French lessons' at the age of 6 in order to make sure that we passed the exams that would get us into the right school. It seems to me that school life did not revolve around targets, tick-box examinations, league tables and endless rounds of 'measuring' standards in ways that tell you very little about what 'learning' or education is going on. Romantic? Maybe. Worrying? Definitely.

The Roots of Wonder

A Christian worldview is shaped by an understanding of God (Creator), of the world/universe (created and self-creating) and of what it means to be human. In the great poem that begins the book of Genesis we read that God brings order out of chaos (metaphorically as well as actually) and that human beings are made in the 'Imago Dei' – the image of God. People are made to cultivate (that is, develop culture in) the world that is given to them as a gift to be cared for, and to reflect in that cultivating the person of the Creator. In this sense, every human being has the innate capacity to know deep inside that there is more to life than merely living and more to know than what is observable. We are born with the profound yearning to know what the person of the Creator is all about in order that we can reflect this in our living and our engagement with the world that is the Creator's gift. In other words, we are made to look beyond ourselves and to not be bound or restricted by the limitations of the observable or the subjectively knowable. There is more. Or, as Augustine put it, 'Our heart is restless till it finds its rest in [God] (*Confessions*)'.

Becoming a Christian

I grew up in a Christian family and from my earliest years had a wider family in the Baptist Church we belonged to in Anfield, Liverpool. My wonderful Sunday School teacher, Mr Chris Keenan, regularly used to ask us if we had asked Jesus into our heart yet. I couldn't quite work out the meaning of this in its metaphysical entirety, but I was eager to please and to be included among the 'acceptable' people. I would reply 'yes' to his question, but not be very sure what I was supposed to have experienced as a result of this invitation. At the age of 11, however, I was taken to a meeting of secondary-school teenagers at the YMCA in Mount Pleasant in Liverpool and listened to an address by a Church Army evangelist about the price Jesus had paid for my sin. That night, after a long conversation with the speaker and a tortuous car journey home, I knelt by my bed and asked Jesus to come into my life and turn me around.

Now, it might sound odd, but my life changed. I knew I was on a different road and my motivation for life-choices had changed (or been changed) for ever. I was 11 and yet I know that something radical happened at that point. I was ignorant of theology, inexperienced in the ways of the world (and struggling to think of which particular sins had made me so 'sinful') and limited in my understanding of life. Nevertheless, from then on I was preoccupied with trying to 'be' a Christian, to understand the Bible, to work out what I should be feeling or experiencing, and to help other people to 'see the light'. For a very long time my theology was concentrated on the sacrifice of Jesus on the cross and the need for people to be saved from the consequences of their sins. It was all about salvation and judgement. Worship seemed (as I recall it) to be centred around thanking God for saving me (never 'us') and telling him how wonderful he was for being so generous. My theology well into my twenties was anthropocentric and probably narcissistic, too – focused on *me, my* experience and *my* eternal destiny.

An Expanding Vision
I will say something later about experiences of growing into adulthood and the theological and spiritual struggles that characterised those years for me, but it will suffice to say here that as my experience of the world grew and expanded and became more complicated, my theology struggled to cope with the tensions produced. An individualistic faith learned in a church which defines itself by its 'independence' from other churches did not help me to face up to the world I was experiencing and learning about through studying other languages and cultures, the politics (and history) of Germany and France, the moral complexity I encountered in the world of military intelligence during the Cold War or the ethical messiness of the lives of the people I was getting to know as I moved around.

In 1984, having been accepted for training for ordination as an Anglican priest, I took my wife and two young children off to Bristol where I would study theology and continue the struggle to make sense of it all. In my first week I was introduced to Rudolf Otto's ruminations on the nature of what is called 'the numinous' in his book *The Idea of the Holy*. Not only did Otto articulate something about the experience of 'otherness', but he opened my eyes for the first time (I think) to the bigger-ness of God and the cosmos. Theology was about more than 'me and God' and 'my salvation'. Some months later I heard Cockburn's *Lord of the Starfields* and began to understand what worship is about. I realised that wonder has to be experienced before worship can be offered and I learned that neither wonder nor worship can be rushed into without having first created the space for contemplation.

The three years I spent at theological college were not easy. I thrived on the study of theology and philosophy, but struggled frequently with the lack of relationship between what went on in the classroom and what went on in the chapel. I found the *self*-centredness of the spirituality difficult to cope with and regret to this day that my personal frustrations found expression in impatience and short-temperedness. I had come from a world of serious moral complexity and ambiguity (intelligence and government) and could not cope with the apparent compartmentalisation that sought to keep theology separate from the 'real' world I felt I had come out of. I have no doubt that my inability to articulate this (partly because of the Official Secrets Act) did not help as I struggled to hold everything together. What I did know, however, was that I could never stand in a pulpit or lead an act of worship if my theology did not cohere and cope with the whole of life, the bigness of God and the universe and the sheer messy reality and complexity of human lives and cultures.

51

Perhaps it was important and maybe even inevitable that my early Christian experience, coinciding as it did with the contradictions and tensions of adolescence, was self-centred. My relationship with God and my eternal destiny were what really concerned me and this concentration had both positive and negative consequences. I was perhaps more serious-minded and focused than many of my friends, but I was also disproportionately worried about my own 'sin' and whether my adolescent urgings were wrong or not. I was worried that if I had a naughty thought on Wednesday, I might be damned to hell by Thursday. I couldn't resolve the tension I saw in other Christians in my church that we had been grasped by a gospel of God's grace (we cannot save ourselves) and then drove ourselves hard to earn God's favour by 'doing it right', obeying the rules and 'believing' the right things.

What this period of my life lacked was the wider vision of God's creative activity and cosmic affection. I think I really believed that the world would end soon anyway (after all, it was the 1970s and the nuclear threat was real) and individual salvation was what mattered. But that did not cope with the wider universe, the Biblical references to the cosmos, the 'cultural mandate' of Genesis 2 or the references to God's love for the whole created order. It was a theological framework that loved working out timetables for the 'end times' and seeing history in terms of 'dispensations', but it did not address the implications of John's vision of a 'new heaven and a new earth' (Revelation 21). The dichotomy between the physical and the spiritual was fairly rigid and anything awkward could be easily spiritualised until the contradiction or conflict/tension seemed less obvious. I simply ducked the questions arising from phrases such as 'that the world might be saved' or 'God so loved the *world* that he gave his only Son ...'.

In one sense, God was shaped in my image: pre-occupied with the minutiae of individual sins, with making sure nothing got past him and tut-tutting about the state of the world and its awful people. Nowhere was to be found the playful celebration of a theology that took creation and covenant as seriously as redemption and salvation.

I now look back and wonder what or who it was we were worshipping. Many of the hymns and songs we sang spoke of a God of the cosmos, but somehow the import of this didn't seem to penetrate into my assumptions about God, the world and me. I cannot speak for others of my contemporaries, but I guess I worshipped a small God who needed to be reminded of what he had done for 'us sinners' and praised for his generosity in sparing us from our deserved fate. This was worship rooted in fear and gratitude, but not expansive enough to recognise the bigness of the God who had created a world that creates itself in a universe of mesmerising and inconceivable size, beauty and complexity. Maybe I was just young and this is how we learn and grow as limited human people, bound to the constraints of the contexts in which we spend our early years. But, maybe the theology I grew up with was also deficient and the view of God a little too definitely tight.

Learning to Worship
The experience of theological college was, however, also nurturing. I began to understand Anglican liturgy and

the reason for liturgy. I had not previously understood the fact that human beings live by repetition of stories and derive their identity from a particular way of telling their communal history. They cultivate corporate or communal rituals to celebrate their story and make sure they do not lose the plot – literally. The Psalms, which were Jesus's hymnbook, address the whole gamut of human emotions and experiences, but the poets responsible for them do not shy away from asking God questions, lamenting their losses, venting their frustrations and offering their thanks. The constant repetition of certain of these poems and songs led eventually to a community of people who knew their story, could articulate it to others and could celebrate it together using a common vocabulary.

Studying theology began to challenge me in a way that many might feel to be ridiculous. In retrospect I would say that I began slowly to realise that I faced a choice between trusting in the God who seemed to become increasingly elusive (because he grew out of the limited dimensions I had unwittingly imposed on him) or holding to a framework of dogmas that would identify me as being 'in' (orthodox) or 'out' (unorthodox). Now, many will say that this is a false dichotomy and that the two must be held together: relationship with God and dogmatic beliefs about him (and all that follows on from such a belief). But the more I studied, the less sure I became that the dogmatic frameworks I had lived with could hold the weight put on them.

I will say more about this later, but the point here is that this movement changed my understanding and experience of worship. To put it simply, as God got bigger and the tight theology became looser, so the questions became more complex and I began to wonder at the enormity of God, his creation and what it means to be human. And it was this wonder that began to reshape worship. I became less patient with endless songs of gratitude to God for what he had done for 'me' and began to use fewer words in marvelling at the God whose concern was never less than 'me', but always bigger than the universe.

During the same period that I was undergoing this transformation, something paradoxical was happening. I trusted God more while worrying less about the detail. And it began to seem clear to me that this is the whole point of theology in the first place – indeed, it is the whole point of the Bible and of worship: to point us to the God who cannot be fully known, but has shown us his face in Jesus of Nazareth. And the Creator of the universe might be a little less worried about the tightness of my theology than he is about the wideness of my creative and costly loving – which is the reflection of who God is anyway.

I found expression of this in the liturgies and songs of the Iona Community and the world church. I met John Bell for the first time when he came to the theological college in Bristol for a day and I was little interested in what he had to say. A Scottish Presbyterian would add to the experience of visiting speakers, but I didn't expect to be inspired any more than usual. However, once again, I was surprised to find myself arrested by being given access to a way of seeing God and the world that held the personal and the communal together and took creation seriously without being miserable, lunatic or just 'worthy'. The liturgies written by John and the Wild Goose Worship Group (as it then was) began with God as Creator and rooted their language in God's implicit love of the material world. No platonic dichotomies between good (spiritual) and bad (material/physical) here then. But this also opened up the possibility of being honest with God and not having to play games with an egomaniac who wants to be praised all the time, even when honesty would bring forth an expression of damning frustration or raging anger.

Furthermore, expression was given to the wonderful bigness of God and the knowable love of a God who is at once above and beyond all that can be imagined, yet also intimately involved in the minutiae of life. Bringing to a predominantly white middle-class English Christian community the expression of worship and wonder that emerges from believers of other cultures and histories was challenging and releasing. It is all too easy to make God in our own image and to attribute to God the limited perceptions or ideals of our own community. Singing the songs of worshippers from other cultures and using other languages rams the point home that God is not a white, middle-aged, middle-class English Anglican.

I will expand on some of this in relation to other matters later in this book, but suffice it to say at this point that the process of rethinking my theology and allowing my prejudices and assumptions to be challenged was not easy. And the best illustration of this experience is still to be found in Genesis 4 in the story of Cain.

Cain kills his brother Abel out of jealousy and is punished by being expelled from the community and land of his family. The text says that he left the land and travelled until he settled in the Land of Nod where

he built a city and called it Enoch. That's pretty well all
we are told. Then the narrative poem moves on. Now,
even as a teenager I read that and wondered what it
was all about. Then, during my time at theological
college I came across a book by a French jurist and
theologian called Jacques Ellul. In *The Meaning of the
City* Ellul suggests that this is meant to be a metaphor of
what it is to be human after all. The poet is attempting
to account for why human beings are the way they are
and to find a way of illustrating it. And that is where
Cain's city comes in.

All human beings feel themselves to be somehow
'at sea' in a desert with no definite points of reference.
If we leave behind the safe place where our identity
(in relation to God, the community and our learned
'story' as human beings) was clear and find ourselves in
a place without boundaries, we have to do something to
'shape our world'. Every human being has a worldview
that puts down (usually unconscious) markers in order
to shrink the enormity of the shapeless expanse and
provide contours within which we can create meaningful
existences. In other words, finding ourselves in the vast
expanse of the desert that is the Land of Nod, we build
some walls and then proceed to construct buildings
or places of meaning and activity within them. Now,
we know who we are and where we are and why we
matter because we have shrunk the enormity of the
uncontrollable universe into something smaller and
more manageable.

What then happens to human beings, however, is
that we begin to mistake the limits (walls) of the city
for the limits of the 'world' or the cosmos. And we
implicitly assume that the world 'out there' is full of

threats and dangers. We must keep the defensive walls of the city as robust as possible and deal firmly with those people who would like to pop outside and see what is out there.

In another book (*Hungry for Hope?*, 2007) I have suggested that these walls get breached by tragedy, bereavement, crisis and death. And we then face a serious choice: (a) we can look through the breach and see a vast expanse of 'world' outside and go out there to explore it – on the assumption that if God is truly God of it all (and not just the bit within our walls), then there is nothing to fear; or (b) we look through the breach, get terrified by the uncertainty of the world out there and rebuild the walls even thicker in order to prevent them being breached again.

And this is the choice I felt I was facing, but from a rather different angle. Rather than it being tragedy or crisis (in the sense described) that provoked this challenge, it was an expanding view of God and an introduction to a different sort of language about God and the world that presented the choice. Yes, there was a crisis in an existential sense around this time, but it went hand in hand with – and possibly emanated from – the challenge that if I truly believe God to be God of everything, then why am I so scared of letting him out of the boxes I had unwittingly put him in? If God cannot be tamed and bound by human limitations (even dogmatic theological limitations), then why can't I go out there from the false security inside the self-made walls of defence and trust him that the uncertainties are not ultimately threatening – that it is more important to learn to trust the God who loves the whole mess of the world than to be able to describe him in detail.

Starfields and Minefields

As we shall see later, to leave the confines of the 'city' and explore the world that bears God's imprint means to see nothing as being beyond his love or his concern. This is why Bruce Cockburn can range so freely between humble worship of the *Lord of the Starfields* through anger against the people who plant the child-killing mines in *Mines of Mozambique* to the intimacy of love for someone in *Live on my Mind*. Wonder does not only lead to worship, but also to engagement with and responsibility for the created world that bears the fingerprints of the Creator. From starfields to minefields to the depths of the human heart, God is to be found. And so are his people.

Chapter 4

RIVER OF TEARS

One of life's great mysteries for me was how on earth anyone ever thought it permissible to allow Boney M to sing *Rivers of Babylon* to a boppy tune. The song is catchy and they managed to stick a chorus in that changed the flow a bit, but the tune and rhythm bear absolutely no relation to the experience alluded to by the lyrics. At least when Don McLean recorded his version 'Babylon' in 1971 it reflected the mood and intention of the original poem by being set in a minor key with a descending mournful melody.

The song is taken from Psalm 137 and is the sort of song that has to be wrenched out of your throat with sobs of horror and pain. It isn't a little ditty that sounds nice when danced to. The story behind the song goes something like this:

The people of Israel, six centuries before Christ, saw their identity tied up inextricably with their possession of the land God had given them after the exodus from Egypt and the forty-year sojourn in the desert. They were God's people and their chosenness gave them status among the nations of the Near East. They knew God was on their side because they lived in the land that had been promised to them. Their history and identity found their vindication in their location. They could sing their songs of praise to their God – who, unusually in the world of the ancient Near East, was not a tribal deity, but the 'Lord' of the cosmos – because they lived with the evidence of God's vindication every day.

However, in the year 587 BC the great Babylonian empire invaded and occupied the land, sending the upper echelons of Israelite society into exile. Sitting by the rivers of the pagan empire, Babylon, how could they possibly sing songs of praise to and proclamation of the God of the whole of creation – God of all the nations – when the evidence of their experience told them with cruel clarity that their God was either non-existent or had just been defeated by the more powerful pagan gods of the invaders? Yet this is what the Babylonian captors were mocking the exiles with: 'Come on, sing your songs now ... while you sit in captivity!' The irony was bitter and the experience tortuous.

Indeed, this wasn't just a slight blip in the story of these people: it was a catastrophe of world-shattering proportions. It wasn't just that a bit of land had been lost and the defeated people upset by a change in their fortunes. Rather, the defeat, loss of land and exile brought the entire worldview of these people crashing to the floor. Had they been conned all along? Was their God in fact weaker than other gods? Had God deserted them or was he, in fact, not there in the first place? All the evidence of their eyes told them that the mockery by the Babylonians was justified and called into question the way the Israelites understood God, the world, history, morality, life and meaning. The exile shattered every bit of certainty the people had ever had.

Now try singing the Boney M song to a boppy tune and a trite rhythm. Then look at the words of Psalm 137, a lament of agonising honesty:

> By the rivers of Babylon we sat and wept when we remembered Zion.
> There on the poplars we hung our harps, for there our captors asked us for songs, our tormentors demanded songs of joy; they said, 'Sing us one of the songs of Zion!' How can we sing the songs of the LORD while in a foreign land?
> If I forget you, O Jerusalem, may my right hand forget its skill. May my tongue cling to the roof of my mouth if I do not remember you, if I do not consider Jerusalem my highest joy.
> Remember, O LORD, what the Edomites did on the day Jerusalem fell. 'Tear it down,' they cried, 'tear it down to its foundations!'
> O Daughter of Babylon, doomed to destruction, happy is he who repays you for what you have done to us – he who seizes your infants and dashes them against the rocks.

Not surprisingly, this Psalm is not often read in church. The prospect of the reader concluding with 'This is the Word of the Lord' and the congregation responding with 'Thanks be to God' seems unappealing. Yet, it should be read – not because the sentiments of the final verse are noble or commendable, but because we need to learn two things: (a) that we are supposed to be honest with God about what we really feel, and (b) that only by using the songs of others do we enter into experiences that might not be ours, but will be those of other people in our community or world. I might feel that life is good, but that is precisely the time I need to enter into the experience of those for whom it isn't. And the corporate worship of the Church should recognise this and recover the Psalms as offering a vocabulary for worship for all people, whatever their circumstances, feelings or faith (or lack of it).

I don't say this glibly. But I recall the brave and perceptive words of a former Bishop of Carlisle, Ian Harland, when he came to conduct a service at the church where I was a curate some years ago. We processed into the church and, on reaching the front, he turned and saw the huge banner stretched from wall to wall along the front of the church balcony: 'You shall go out with joy!' it ordered, with colourful balloons added for emphasis. The banner had been there for a long time, so I had ceased noticing it. The bishop saw it for the first time and asked what it said to those who came into church feeling that their life was falling apart or that God was not there. What, he asked me later, did we expect someone to do if they felt something other than joy at the end of a service: go out pretending (not very honest), or feel that they must have done something wrong to not feel joyful? He was not being a miserable killjoy; rather, he was fulfilling his vocation which was to see the pastoral implications of what was being said and to ask the right question at the right time.

I also remember being part of a group of clergy who were asked to note our favourite traditional hymn and modern worship song. We then pushed them through a grid made up of the sort of expressions that represent the gamut of emotions and behaviours that form part of close human relationships. Few, if any, hymns and songs could be said to complain to God, ask God questions, lament our circumstances, voice our more unpleasant desires (à la Psalm 137) or leave our desires unmet. In other words, our worship was partial and limited – usually to those things we thought God would like to hear from us. At the time I found this deeply challenging to my own way of choosing songs and hymns for church services, for I realised that I was probably depriving whole groups of people of the opportunity to worship and engage with God honestly. I realise that not everybody can be catered for in a single act of worship, but when I looked back over the previous three months I felt more than embarrassed. Where would the woman whose child had died find space and language for 'worship'? Where would the man whose wife had left him for someone else find himself acknowledged and his experienced recognised? Where would the teenager abused by a leader find her own experience given even subtle expression and know herself to be heard by God and his people? These are not theoretical cases.

The Blues

Gospel music has its origins in the experience of the black slaves in America. Rock 'n' roll derived from black music and gave expression to all the things you wouldn't sing about in church. Instead of sanitised or guilt-inducing theology, post-Second World War rock music opened up the whole of human experience to public acknowledgement and validated the expression of the darker sides of life. The complexities of relationships could be explored and the inconsistencies of human life expressed in language and music that many people found both releasing and realistic. Real experience was

65

accepted and it is perhaps this, more than anything else, which began the drift of young people from the churches. If God (or the Church) cannot cope with reality, why bother?

This is deeply ironic. The slave music came out of the experience of oppression and the conviction that the God of justice who delivered the Israelites from captivity in Egypt would one day deliver them from their own 'exile'. It was rooted in an acknowledgement of bereavement and held onto the hope that loss would be followed by new possibilities – our vindication will come, even if we have to wait generations to see it. Surely it was the Church above all other institutions that should have been able not only to cope with the reality of people's complicated lives, but proactively to give expression to it? Well, maybe.

The blues gave expression to the downside of life and the unresolved passions and experiences of ordinary people living in the real world. BB King, Sonny Terry, John Lee Hooker and others poured out both the joy and the grief of real people's lives and made them resonate through sublime rhythm and melody. George Harrison's guitar might well have weeped gently, but the descending, unresolving chords and plaintive melodies of the blues somehow evoked the unarticulated emotions of many people whose lives were not as the Church would like them to be. The inconsistencies of sexual behaviour, love and loss could be explored without apology or embarrassment in songs of unashamed grief or celebration. The blues seem to speak of what *is* rather than what *should be*.

Call me selective if you wish, but the prime exponent of the blues for me is Eric Clapton. Having listened to his records over the years, I was still unprepared for the agonising beauty of *Pilgrim*, released on CD in 1998. Not only did the album contain songs about loss and his relationship with his unknown father (*My Father's Eyes*), but also the wonderful lament that is *River of Tears*. This song speaks of loss and shame and regret and hope, but it is the understated guitar playing and the haunting sadness of Clapton's voice which makes you long to know what caused the song to be written. What was the pain of the separation that gave birth to such beautiful sadness and such a dreadful yearning? This is the lament of someone who has made the same mistakes before and who resigns himself to the inevitability of repeated loss.

I love the blues, and this song in particular, not because I am miserable, but because the searing honesty of it screams out and resonates. It is not always possible to be honest in the Church because there are always people who can only cope with your drowning in your own tears if you then resolve the problem by 'finding Jesus'. Unfortunately, life is not always like that; fortunately, neither is Jesus – but that will have to wait for a later chapter.

I think I need at this point to get personal and explain why the blues strike something in me that does not resonate anywhere else. In my experience, there are those who assume that a bishop has had an easy ride through the years, being an innate 'believer' who has simply continued on the upward escalator of life and faith until he found himself privileged to exercise religious power in the institution of the Church. Obviously, such a person never has doubts and has never had to grapple with the internal contradictions of living as a Christian in the 'real' world. Well, I am afraid that if it is true of others, it certainly isn't true of me. What has been called the 'dark night of the soul' – the absence of God – has been a regular companion of mine for decades and throughout my Christian life.

Germany

When I was 19, I went to work in a town near Stuttgart in what was then West Germany. As part of my university course in modern languages I had to spend a year working in industry, not going to parties at foreign universities as many language students seemed to do in those days. I worked for six months with a freelance technical translator in a village called Spraitbach, a few kilometres north of a town called Schwäbisch Gmünd. I loved the work, but outside of the work I rented a room in a large house and found the whole lonely experience extremely difficult. I had recently become engaged to Linda and had been in hospital for surgery. Leaving England was neither a welcome nor an easy experience for me. Whereas most of my fellow students seemed to be eager to get away and enjoy the year ahead, I dreaded it. Contrary to appearances, I was not self-confident and (ridiculous though it seems now) I didn't know if Linda would wait for me to return – a reflection on my insecurity, not her fickle affections.

What made it worse for me was that I had always belonged to a Christian community of some sort and never really been away from one for any length of time. I belonged to a large youth group in a Baptist church in Liverpool before going to university, where

I joined the Christian Union and found myself (much to my surprise) worshipping in an Anglican church in Bradford, West Yorkshire. I had been involved in small groups of young Christians studying the Bible and trying to be creative in outreach and evangelism. Intellectually, I was stimulated and was happy to have my mind stretched by the study of European history, languages, philosophy and culture. My theology was secure and I knew what I believed about God, the world and me.

Being wrenched from all this while also recovering from surgery caused more of a shock than I ever anticipated. I worked in the basement office of my boss's home in Spraitbach and saw no one during the day other than him (when he was there) and his family. In the evening I would get the bus back down into town and go straight to my rented room at the top of the house. Most nights I would simply get into bed and try to sleep in order to shut out the loneliness and sense of isolation. The only thing that kept me there and kept me going was the family I met at a small local church; they showed me friendship and extraordinary generosity in return for which I gave them my misery. They probably have no idea how important they were to my survival during those months, but the Semraus are still friends now – three decades later.

This was the first time I really questioned my faith. All the assumptions I had grown up with were exposed in the experience of loneliness. I wondered if God was there at all and found myself, probably for the first time, prepared to throw the whole Christian thing in. I had to let go of the fear that rejecting God or Christianity would leave me bereft, and engage with the serious intellectual and existential questions I had thus far managed to contain. I remember coming to the conclusion one evening that I could not carry on as I had been – that if it was really only the social milieu of my upbringing that made me conform to Christian commitment and belief, I could not continue in that way. Integrity demanded that I face the hard questions and act consistently on the answers, however comfortable or uncomfortable they might prove to be. Clearly, for some people this would not be such a big deal; but for me it was potentially world-shattering.

In 1978, after six months in Germany, I returned to England for six weeks and then went out to work in Paris for six months. After just three months of living in a hostel, working for a telecommunications company and getting arrested for busking on the Metro, I had to return to England for further medical treatment. Three months later and I was back out in Paris again for several months before returning to university for the final stretch. During this time the questioning went on and went deep. I must have been awful to live with and I cannot remember those couple of years being characterised by fun and laughter. With university over, Linda and I got married and moved to Cheltenham where I was to retrain as a Russian linguist for the British Government at its Communications Headquarters (GCHQ). Married life was accompanied by the interest of learning a new language and a new 'trade' and we got involved with an Anglican church, helping with the youth work.

Whatever else appeared to be going on during this time, I was seriously questioning the meaning of life, God and 'meaning' itself. And it wasn't making me particularly happy. This wasn't simply a matter of intellectual interest or existential indifference; I could not escape the fact that the conclusions I drew would have to drive my identity and my ethics. I had little patience with people who claim a particular religious or philosophical commitment, but then live as if different rules apply. To put it bluntly, if God is not there and Jesus is just an interesting historical character, then there are serious implications for how I orientate my life, make my choices, value relationships and things. Conversely, if God truly is there (whatever that might look like), there would be serious implications for my life, choices, etc. So, this was not a trivial matter for me.

Iona

Fast-forward a few years to a different place. The time in Cheltenham had seen me wrestle with some of these questions and come to certain conclusions. I had left GCHQ in 1984, having been accepted for ordination training in the Church of England. This had not been an easy decision as it meant giving up my profession, moving my family into a different way of life and losing our home. But I had not been able to shake off the nagging voice that kept me dissatisfied with what I felt was just 'doing a job'. I felt I wanted to make a difference in the world and have an opportunity to be creative rather than reproductive. (Linguists can find themselves always dealing with other people's ideas.) Once I had been accepted for training, Linda and I decided we needed another year in what we rudely called 'the real world' before moving to Bristol to start the course.

I could not have done this had I not been clear that I was a Christian and would devote my life to serving the world through the Church as an ordained minister. We moved to Bristol in 1984 and I began studying theology academically. The big shock here came from having the theological frameworks I had just about recovered (albeit in reshaped form) questioned again. As I have indicated earlier, I struggled with elements of this college experience – largely because of the tensions created by the professional environment I had come from – but I soon began to enjoy the freedom to question and to explore theology and philosophy in conjunction with exposure to communities of people I had hitherto ignored (such as probationers in a bail hostel whom I visited once a week as part of my course).

All seemed to be going well until the beginning of the final straight in the third year. Intellectually, I was convinced of God and a Christian worldview, but I was better able to live with 'grey areas' and to be less intense about ultimate meaning. I had relaxed in friendships and was more at peace within myself – able to let other people 'be' without wanting to change them. The things that had driven me to distraction about worship cultures (why do people sing about 'falling down on my knees in worship' while standing up with their arms in the air?) didn't worry me so much any longer. I felt more relaxed and spiritually stronger than I had done for many years. And then, inexplicably, the world came crashing down.

One Friday evening in March, three months before I was due to move my family up north to the Lake District and be ordained in Carlisle Cathedral, I reluctantly stayed in college for Evening Prayer. A friend whose husband was training with me came in for the service which most students were trying to get out of attending. Afterwards I asked her why. She explained that, having not prayed or looked at the Bible for months, she had been sitting in bed the night before, reflecting on all they had, when she became overwhelmed with gratitude to God. The power of this spiritual experience had surprised her and she wasn't in a position fully to explain it. I listened and then went to collect my bike for the three-mile ride home. But instead of getting on the bike, I went to my study and sat and wept. I was there for over an hour, weeping and feeling desolate. And I had no idea why and I couldn't control it.

That began a weekend in which I wondered if I could carry on and continue to call myself a Christian, let alone be ordained. I felt in the depths of my soul an emptiness and sense of dereliction that I had never experienced before and have never experienced since. I had a loving wife, two young children and a third on the way; I was about to embark on a lifelong ministry mediating the love and grace of God to people I had not yet encountered; I was physically fit and had everything going for me; I had even discovered Bruce Cockburn and some other wonderful artists; yet I felt desolate. I spent the weekend in tears.

The following week was a mess. I struggled through college lectures and seminars, saved only by a member of staff who seemed to understand what was happening and tried neither to 'resolve' it, nor give me glib answers to my predicament. On the Wednesday I forced myself to attend an evening Eucharist in the college chapel – a service that went on for three hours. People were encouraged to ask God for charismatic experiences and 'anointings' and I felt the dreadful inevitability of having to ask others to pray for me. They did. Nothing happened. I would have danced naked on the altar if God would promise to make himself inescapably evident to me in some way; but nothing happened and I went home in a worse state to that in which I had arrived. Where was God when I needed some affirmation? And why did other people seem to get all the 'confirming' experiences of intimacy with God, whereas I did not?

A couple of days later I took an overnight train to Glasgow and then a string of buses and boats to reach the tiny remote island of Iona, in the Inner Hebrides of Scotland. This is where St Columba had landed prior to his missionary travels in Britain which helped bring Christianity to the pagans. I had only come to Iona because someone else had paid for me to attend a theological students' week with the Iona Community and I felt too embarrassed to pull out at this late stage. Before I left home in Bristol I told my wife that if nothing had changed by the time I returned, I would have to leave college and not go ahead with the ordination. She then had a week with the children not knowing if her life would change radically when I eventually returned. This was serious stuff and I wouldn't want to defend the tactless insensitivity of my handling of elements of that situation.

Iona is so remote that there is no point trying to run away. Unfortunately, the abbey's heating system had just broken down and it was freezing cold. And the content of the week wasn't what I had expected. Nevertheless, there was little alternative but to join in and try to get something out of it. I felt miserable and spiritually empty. And then something changed.

I had started keeping a journal and I used the free time on Iona to write. I poured out my feelings and thoughts with more honesty than I had ever ventured to express before. The pages filled up, coloured by conversations with John Bell and Graham Maule who were leading the week. On the Wednesday it was the responsibility of the guests to order and lead worship in the ancient abbey. I felt in no fit state even to contribute to this; there was simply too much 'stuff' going on in my head and my heart and I decided to keep my head down.

The day was spent on a pilgrimage around the island, visiting the places where St Columba had used the land to help shape his community of evangelising monks so many centuries before. This bleak place is where Columba and his fellows had brought Christianity to northern Britain – of course, not actually knowing when they arrived that they would be beginning the conversion of this North Atlantic island. At one end of the isle there is what is known as the 'Hermit's Cell'. Now it is just a circle of stones, but Columba used it for housing the difficult, cantankerous or unsociable monks who needed time out and away from everyone else. Living in a close community is not an easy experience and this offered a practical solution when problems arose and space was needed. If you come here as part of the pilgrimage, you will be asked to keep silence until you have climbed the hill and the cell is no longer in sight. In the silence all you can hear is the wind and the sea and the calling of birds. I sat there and also perceived the 'still, small voice' that spoke of God.

In the evening the service in the abbey began in total darkness with me singing a song of dereliction, asking

God to touch me in the night time of my emptiness with hands of healing. I cannot explain what had changed, but I felt – for the first time in ages – at peace. Oddly, I felt I had given up the struggle and it didn't matter. God, if he is there, must be big enough to cope with me and my limitations and inconsistencies and my experienced-shaped personality. I cannot say I felt God to be closer or that I had a great spiritual experience or that God had finally looked me in the eye and said 'hello'. I have tried over the last twenty years to find the words that would describe or explain what had actually happened that day on Iona, but I can't. Some things cannot be expressed or rationalised – like trying to put 'beauty' in a test-tube and analyse its make-up. All I know is that something changed and I could live with the 'distance' of God, knowing that I am loved and that this is all that matters.

I tell this story because I think most Christians experience something similar to what I have described. If some people find that their normal experience is of the manifest and incontrovertible close intimacy of God's presence, then I am pleased for them and hope to see evidence of this in their lives. But I know too many Christians who feel somehow inadequate because they cannot honestly use the language of intimacy to describe their relationship with God. Some people get easily moved by spiritual experiences; some of us only very rarely have such glimpses of God. For many of us the 'normal Christian life' is one in which God often seems to be quiet or even absent and we get on with serving him out of obedience and conviction. But it seems to me that this is OK. After all, when the disciples tried to hold on to Jesus after the resurrection, he disappeared and made them just get on with it.

What these experiences (and there have been others) have done is to stop me worrying about where God is and what I feel about him. God's people have – from the very outset in Eden – been called to show the world what God is like and to give their lives in order that God's character might be seen and touched in some way. In other words, the presence and character of God must be 'made flesh' in order for people to recognise them. And part of this has to do with being honest about the whole of life's experience, whatever that brings. A spirituality that only works in Wimbledon, but not Baghdad, is not worth having; it is a delusion. A theology that only 'works' when things go well is a denial of the life which God fully entered in Jesus of Nazareth. If God opts into the complex and often cruel world, then his people must do the same – even when it leads to them screaming honestly from a place of crucifixion: 'My God, why have you abandoned me?' (Matthew 27:46).

Helmut Thielicke was a German theologian and pastor who, sadly, is little known outside of Germany now. During the Second World War his church in Hamburg was bombed and many of his congregation killed. Standing at the edge of the bomb crater amid the ruins of a building where God had been worshipped, he refused to run away from the challenge of the 'where is God in this?' question. Bombed out of his own home, he walked with his family through the streets of a village looking for emergency quarters. Having been bombed out of the city of Hamburg, they found themselves in this village where no bombs had fallen and people were civil. In a sermon published as 'Jesus Christ in the Front-line Trenches' (in *Christ and the Meaning of Life*, James Clarke & Co, London, 1965) Thielicke spoke of his surprise at not feeling relieved by this 'normality': He felt ostracised and tormented by the tranquility. The problem was that the people in this village had not experienced the violent terror and loss that Thielicke and his family had just endured and, therefore, could not understand it.

He explains how he felt most at home back in the ruined city where people bore the scars of terror and fear. Why? Because these people had suffered and therefore understood that Thielicke had gone through.

He goes on to describe how it is the poets who are the true contemporary pastors. Poets do not hand out easy solutions, but give searingly honest expression to despair and dread. Wounded people are helped by those who also have been wounded.

Thielicke goes on to speak of how God has come among us in Jesus, come down to the front-line trenches where the suffering is acute and where God is both longed for and despised for being absent. Yet – and this is the scandal of Christianity – it is precisely here that God is to be found: where Eric Clapton's 'river of tears' runs deepest.

This raises questions for me about both some popular theology and the nature of our churches. I know churches where Thielicke would feel at home in his dereliction and the clergy who lead and serve such churches (and parishes) are utterly wonderful. But no one will write books about these churches because the work is hard, relentless and often unrewarding. There is no glamour and there are few glory stories. People make progress and then profoundly disappoint, but the river does not stand still and life carries on and the church is still there for all the casualties of modern life and loss.

I do not wish to criticise those churches that appear to be 'successful', however that should be defined. But I do want to call our churches back to being places where the whole of our human experience can be lived with, expressed, owned without embarrassment, articulated and embraced. These should be communities where reconciliation and healing can be offered, but the welcome not be withdrawn when neither takes place. These should be spaces where the wounded can slowly discover that the risen Christ, rather than wiping out all evidence of pain and the horrors of human experience, still bears the wound marks of his torture and crucifixion. In other words, our churches should be places where the blues find a place, where the wounded find welcome by people who know their own woundedness and are not embarrassed about it.

More particularly, they must be places where poets are welcome. (Given some of the internal battles going on in churches, it seems we prefer lawyers to poets.) It must be deeply ironic that people find resonance with Clapton's 'river of tears' outside the community that seems not to offer such articulation of honest emotion and experience, when the raison d'être of this community is precisely to hold out wounded hands to the world. For myself, all I can say is that facing up to the 'absence' of God in the experiences I have described, changed my ministry and my priorities, causing me to read the familiar Bible with newly opened eyes and a refreshed hunger for reality.

I follow Jesus because I am sure that he is (as the writer of the letter to the Christians at Colossae puts it in 1:15) the 'image [literally, 'icon'] of the invisible God'. What I *feel* no longer feels so important.

Chapter 5

THE TIMES THEY ARE A-CHANGIN'

One of the things that really irritates you when you are young is the habit of older people (that is, older than 30 …) to talk romantically (and selectively) about the past and to bemoan all the changes that have taken place since their own childhood. When you are young you assume this is because older people have stopped living and only have the past to entertain them. You think they are jealous of the opportunities younger people have today and want simply to stop you enjoying yourself.

Well, maybe they are right. But it needs to be said that it has ever been thus and, in this sense, there is nothing new under the sun. Furthermore, it is surely inevitable that the longer you live, the more you have to reflect upon and the more stories you have to tell. And anyone will tell you that the older you get, the more amazed you become that you have ever got to where you are. Life is full of choices, challenges, opportunities, frustrations, gifts and serendipities, but we never know how it is all going to work out. So, there is no substitution for living it and every 'living' is unique, bringing its own unique stories to be told. Young people will discover the journey only as they travel on their own particular road. Then, one day, they

81

will find themselves doing what they always promised they wouldn't: bemoaning the changes in the world, worrying about 'the young people' and reminiscing about 'the good old days'.

All this demonstrates is the truism that time never stands still. And because nothing stands still, things move on and we are called upon to create the world as we go. We cannot reflect on the journey without having actually done the journey in the first place. So, nothing remains the same.

It was impossible to grow up in the latter part of the twentieth century and escape the penetrating poetry of Bob Dylan. I hated his voice when I was younger and this deterred me from listening to his music ... until I heard *A Hard Rain's A-Gonna Fall* and *Masters of War* (*The Freewheelin' Bob Dylan*, 1963) and realised that he had put into words what I wanted to express about my fear of and for the world, but couldn't. Read his lyrics and he comes over as both a poet and prophet – for example, singing of climate change and ecological threats decades before these became seen as urgent. Dylan fearlessly rampages through the sensibilities and experiences of his generation, exposing the humbug, nailing the pretensions of the powerful and celebrating the realities of life as a growing man.

Since discovering the powerful indictment of *A Hard Rain's A-Gonna Fall* I have come to love the rawness of his voice and the challenge of his words. Dylan seems to have gone through every experience life can throw at us as human beings and most of it is charted through his songs. Despite being called a 'Judas' when he betrayed the acoustic generation by turning electric and bringing a band with him, he just kept trying out new ways of making his music. His songs expose the constant searching for meaning and understanding that drove him through a variety of philosophies and commitments. When he explored Christianity he confronted the dismissive sneers of offended secular liberalism by writing and singing about his new faith in several albums. It was as if he was working it all out through his music and songwriting, exploring in poetry the implications of his new-found worldview in simple and blunt language. He appropriated some old clichéd evangelical Christian language and played with it – almost as if he could test it out in this way and see how far it would hold.

Well, he has since moved on and would probably not now call himself a Christian. But Christian language and motifs keep creeping into his songs, almost as if they have become part of him and cannot help but seep out. In his wonderful 2006 album *Modern Times* he sings about his king (*Thunder on the Mountain*) and alludes to the biblical imaging of the Spirit moving on the face of the waters in creation (*Spirit on the Water*) as he blends creation with a confusing relationship. He sums up the human condition as we face death in the light of our inconsistent lives with a reference to Jesus' crown of thorns (*When the Deal Goes Down*). Dylan has been shaped by all that has happened to him and through him, but refuses to sanitise it or shape his music to please people who want him to stand still and be the man they want him to be. He has the naked courage of the prophet who can make us laugh with pleasure, weep with sadness and shake our fists at the world before then holding up a mirror in which we are confronted by our hypocrisies and fear-driven insecurities. He is not always comfortable to be with.

What Dylan recognises clearly is that today is tomorrow's yesterday (*The Times They Are A-Changin'*) – that we are creating today what will tomorrow be regarded as history. Or memory?

Memory and History

At the beginning of 2008 I delivered a public lecture at the invitation of the Department for Sustainable Heritage at the University of London on the theme of 'time, place and identity' (although the title I chose was a bit more embarrassingly trite than this). During my preparation I read some interesting material by the Chief Rabbi of the United Hebrew Congregations of the Commonwealth (based in the UK), Sir Jonathan Sacks, on the subject of 'memory and history'. He picked up on the notion that memory belongs to the living and that this eventually becomes 'history' when there is no one for whom the memory is 'live'. For example, as the last survivors of the First World War die out, the memories also disappear and 'history' is what we (who have no direct memory of it) do to shape and make sense of events in someone else's past. He observes that history relates dates and events whereas memory invokes a narrative in which we live and have place, identity and significance. He suggests that 'history' is about somewhere else and events elsewhere, whereas 'memory' is about 'me' and my story. History, deals with questions about dates and events, but memory questions identity itself: who am I?

This view is consistent with the Jewish notion of what we might call 'liturgical remembering' as a 're-telling as if we were there' (for example, in the celebration of the Passover) rather than an intellectual acknowledgement that something significant happened a long time ago. And this view is powerful, recognising that memory has to be kept alive as far as possible for the sake of the community that has been shaped by the events remembered.

However, the Croatian theologian, Miroslav Volf (who in 2008 was teaching at Yale in the United States), is not seduced by this. Whereas Sacks will inevitably be haunted by the Jewish experience of the Holocaust and the contemporary fear that this will be forgotten or denied, Volf comes from a part of Europe (the Balkans) where memories have become instruments – even justifiers – of violence, bitterness and dispossession. He maintains that memories can be selective, romantic, destructive or victim-led, and be appropriated in such a way as to give apparent legitimacy to a current grievance because of past offence or suffering (Kosovo, Rwanda, Israel-Palestine). Given that we can never identify the point where a particular 'history' began, we need also to learn how to forget. Memory, according to Volf, cannot be ignored, but it can be handled in a constructive way – forgiveness – that enables people to move beyond the pain and loss into a new freedom. Forgiveness allows both the victim and the perpetrator to find (as in the message of the Old Testament prophets) hope for a new beginning, a new relationship. The past is not ignored; it is faced and accepted, but at considerable cost. After all, freedom never comes cheap.

The tension between Sacks and Volf is instructive. The Truth and Reconciliation Commission in post-apartheid South Africa was a brave attempt to take seriously the need to face the past in order to remove its sting and open up a future. Victims and the families of victims of violence were invited to meet the perpetrators of crimes, but only where both parties agreed to tell the truth and to listen to each other express their mind and heart. This led to some agonisingly painful encounters in which people met the men who had tortured and murdered their loved ones – on both sides of the racial and political divide. They had to listen to indescribably awful depictions of events that cried out for justice. They had to look into the eyes of those who had irrevocably changed their lives and caused unspeakable loss. And they had to decide whether or not to forgive. Memory had to be faced and then choices had to be made.

Whether with individuals or whole communities, the dilemma is painfully real. Do we condemn future generations – our children and grandchildren and their children and grandchildren – to further horrors and injustices in the future because we cannot deal with our own grief today? These are not easy questions and this is not the place to embark on a treatise on the dangers of what Dietrich Bonhoeffer referred to as 'cheap grace', but it illustrates the importance for human identity of the stories that (a) have shaped us and (b) we choose to shape the particular memory/history/identity we wish to appropriate. Inevitably, of course, all stories are selective and partial.

Experiencing Change

It has been said that the act of remembering is literally re-membering: putting back together the elements (members) of the story that give it coherence and significance. It involves a retelling of a narrative that gives shape to the past, either explains or justifies the present and gives direction to the future. Another way of putting it might be: we can only shape our future if we know who and where we are now; and we can only know who and where we are now if we know where we have come from and how we came to be who and where we are now. The problem, however, is that the looking back is easier than not knowing what lies ahead and the looking back is not a straightforward exercise.

The main national monument in Jakarta, Indonesia, is called Monas (Monumen Nasional). It is a 137-metre tower offering a great view through the smog over the expansive city. Apart from going up it, you can also go downstairs underneath the tower and visit the exhibition about the country's Declaration of Independence which was secured on 17 August 1945. The four sides of the basement contain a number of dioramas apparently showing the history of Indonesia going back to prehistoric times when boats sailed over to Java from Sumatra. What is odd about this is that these prehistoric boats are topped with the post-Independence flag of modern Indonesia. So, the whole exhibition is designed to justify how Indonesia has become what it is today and is clearly not designed to be honest or historical in any sense (though pretending to be so).

But whether we read back in history or look forward to the future we cannot escape the fact that change cannot be avoided. Every day, every week, every year brings new challenges and opportunities for anyone with a pulse. Time does not stand still and wait for us to take a break from the relentless progress of anno domini. Clearly, for some people change is threatening, whereas for others it is the source of promise and hope. Perhaps the greatest deficit in the way we bring up our children is our failure to give them strategies for coping with constant change – much of it beyond their control to change. Whereas 'change management' is being recognised as crucial in the business and commercial worlds (and, increasingly, in the churches), we do little to help our children understand how things change and how change is to be addressed in its different guises.

Linda and I got married in 1980 and as we stood at the front of the church making our vows, we had no idea what lay before us. We might make it into retirement and live to be centenarians. On the other hand, one of us might get cancer in our thirties and leave the partner widowed. There were no guarantees that our hopes and aspirations would be fulfilled. We made our vows with complete integrity and intention, but standing at the front of the church was probably not the time or place to philosophise miserably about all the things that might militate against fulfilment. The title of the great Bruce Cockburn song *Anything Can Happen* sums up the unpredictability of life (in which he mocks those who try to avoid any insecurity and fear all the things that could possibly go wrong).

Linda and I moved to Cheltenham where she began nursing and I retrained as a Russian linguist. I had studied and worked in German and French, but now had the opportunity to learn a new language and work in the hidden world of government intelligence. When on day one I, along with nine others in my group, confronted the Cyrillic alphabet for the first time, I had no expectation other than that I would now realise my ambition to be a professional linguist in an interesting world.

Eighteen months later we had our first child, Richard, and I was enjoying my work – now operational rather than training. I was never a natural linguist like some of my colleagues. I had to work at it and lacked the natural flair that good linguists demonstrate. I was better on paper than orally and was beginning to learn my limitations as well as my strengths. But my interest in the complexities of international politics and conflict was deepening and becoming better informed. Professionally and intellectually this was usually very stimulating and sometimes very challenging to the assumptions and prejudices I brought to my view and understanding of the world and why it is the way it is.

As I have indicated earlier, this was also the time I was having to work through my faith anew. What I had become clear about was that faith and theology have to be integrated in a worldview that is credible in what I rudely used to call 'the real world'. A theology that stood *alongside* the experience of the world was a fantasy. A theology that could not be explained credibly in the real world was not worth having. But the world outside was changing and that brought certain threats to global stability: the Soviet occupation of Afghanistan continued, the Argentinians invaded the Falkland Islands in the South Atlantic and the Solidarity trade union was growing in strength in Poland. The old orders still looked pretty solid, but there appeared to be no end in sight to the conflict in Northern Ireland, and the post-Second World War map of the world looked fairly stable: the pink bits looked unlikely to change.

But the world I took for granted as the starting point was, of course, radically different from that of my parents and grandparents who had endured the decline of the British Empire and two catastrophic wars. The map I took as 'normal' was the product of vast redrawings during previous decades.

I suppose we all measure change from some point in our lives or consciousness that we assume to be a sort of base-line. I say 'assume' because we don't rationally argue for the adoption of this 'reality' – we unconsciously assume it and then work from it. When I left government service in 1984 I was seeing the rise of a more confident and militant Islam in the Middle East and parts of Africa and Asia; but I had no idea that the Soviet Union and its satellite states in Eastern Europe were only five years away from total collapse. After the fall of the Soviet Union the USA remained the only global superpower and exploited that role in disturbing ways, seeing itself as the God-ordained global policeman. The events of 11 September 2001 would, at that point, have been unthinkable let alone unpredictable. The economic rise of China and India would equally have seemed unlikely. If it appeared that mass migration had ended after the horrors of the Second World War, then it was shocking to see millions of people moving around Africa, Central Europe and Asia in the wake of new wars, climate change and ethnic conflict.

As I write this, in 2008, we still do not know what will happen to the occupation of Iraq, the tensions with Iran, a resurgent Russia, a China annoyed by international reaction to human rights abuses and the occupation of Tibet, the Israeli–Palestinian struggle, and so on. We write history as if events were consequent on what had gone before, but the reality is that order is usually lacking and consistency is identified more by coincidence than design on the part of governments and leaders.

The same phenomenon can be observed in one's own personal experience. I am not the same person I was when my wife agreed to marry me. I have been changed by time and the experiences we have either enjoyed or endured during the last thirty years. Our three children have very different personalities and have begun to find their own ways through life in their own unique ways. But the world they have grown up in is not the one I knew when I was young. The information explosion and IT revolution have radically changed the shape of the world for them, and the possibilities for international travel are greater (and cheaper) and more accessible than they ever were for me. In one sense, I can't imagine what the world looks or sounds like when seen through their eyes and heard through their ears. Music has changed, film/media have changed and popular culture bears no resemblance to that of my youth. And, of course, for millions of their contemporaries around the world these changes have brought not an expansion of opportunity, but an increase in conflict, poverty, exploitation and migration.

I have conducted the weddings of two of my children. Standing with them at the front of the churches I pondered on what might lie ahead of them. Nothing is inevitable, but lots of things are possible. Yet, what is most clear is that they will create their futures by the choices they make as they go along. Only later, after many years, will they know whether or not some of these choices were the right ones or the wrong ones. Only in retrospect will they regret missed opportunities and celebrate the life they have ended up with. Perhaps maturity consists in accepting who you have become and where you have come to in life and not wasting energy wishing you were something, someone or somewhere else.

The Two Halves of Life

Richard Rohr, the American Franciscan priest who founded the Center for Action and Contemplation in Albuquerque, New Mexico, in 1986, is becoming increasingly well-known in Europe. I heard him speak at the Greenbelt Arts Festival in Cheltenham in 2005, but went only reluctantly. The speaker I wanted to listen to had cancelled (I think) and I went with my wife and a couple of friends to sit on the grass in the sun while Rohr did his thing. I started to read my book, intending to use the time profitably, but was distracted by his introductory remarks and then couldn't stop listening. His theme was 'the two halves of life'.

Rohr described the first half of life (defined not by chronology, but by maturity) as being dominated by what he called 'the container'. Great attention is given, he says, to the shape and form of the container. This is why young people look for clarity of boundaries and why religious young people want black and white dogmas – orthodoxies that either include or exclude people from particular communities. But, says Rohr, the second half of life is characterised not by preoccupation with the container itself, but rather with the *contents* of it. In other words, we relax about the rigidities of the container and concentrate more on the substance of life and living. Of course, this is partly because the second half of life is lived with a growing sense of mortality, a sense that not everything can be put off for the future. This can lead to a greater preoccupation with living for today (in its best sense) rather than directing both energy and resources towards an as-yet-undetermined future.

It seemed to me listening to Richard Rohr that he had just described one of the changes I felt I had been experiencing for some time. I was becoming increasingly impatient with the churchy obsession with drawing lines in the sand and was increasingly taken with the people who encountered Jesus in the gospels – people whose lives were often messy and who found an embrace in the person of Jesus, usually to the concern of the religious leaders who knew 'how to be godly'. Jesus may have been only in his early thirties when he was crucified outside Jerusalem, but he was clearly in the 'second half of life' as described by Richard Rohr.

Dr Richard Burridge, Dean of Kings College, London, has drawn out a similar thread from a study of Jesus and ethics. In his *Imitating Jesus: An Inclusive Approach to New Testament Ethics* (Eerdmans, 2007), he describes how the reader of the gospels must resist isolating Jesus's ethical teaching from the account of how he then actually dealt with people. To accentuate the former at the expense of the latter is to distort the picture and misunderstand both Jesus himself and the intentions of the gospel writers. Burridge observes that Jesus accentuated or radicalised the demands of the Old Testament law to the extent that they cannot be fulfilled by ordinary human beings. Jesus was clear, uncompromising and allowed for no dilution in his teaching about what behavioural standards would reflect the character of the God in whose image we are made. But, says Burridge, you then have to go on to look at how Jesus related to the very people who failed abysmally to meet the standards he had proclaimed: he consistently defended them against the condemnations of the legalistic pedants who wanted to apply the law with enthusiastic precision; he also offered them an acceptance characterised by a generosity and forgiveness that set them free from the failures that bound them and let them start again.

Burning Desire

Change is not just something that happens to us despite our resistance to it; it is a phenomenon of being alive that should be embraced and enjoyed. When Bono sang with passion of the burning desire within him he was describing the power of sexual desire and the need to be loved. This comes in the middle of his great song 'I Still Haven't Found What I'm Looking For' (*The Joshua Tree*, 1987) and beautifully expresses the reality that most human beings have within them a constant desire for 'more' and 'better'. What I mean by this is simply that we change because we grow and because the world (and people) around us changes and grows. So, the context in which we live and relate and choose and desire constantly changes in ways that make us change too. And it is this yearning that demands honesty, whatever the 'right' answers we are supposed to give. Bono still hasn't found what he is looking for, despite his love for God and his wife, and he isn't afraid to demonstrate what it feels like.

I remarked earlier that I am not the same person I was when my wife married me, but nor is she the same woman I married all those years ago. I was planning to be a professional linguist and she was a nurse. Thirty years later and I am an Anglican bishop who writes, broadcasts and does a million other interesting and challenging things. Linda not only does community nursing, but also is an artist working mainly in stained glass – something neither of us would have conceived as being possible all those years ago. The genius of a long relationship is to recognise that we change within it and are changed by it in ways we cannot predict; but we change together in ways that liberate and recognise that there will always be a 'burning desire' for 'more' and 'other'. That is how we are made.

Light at the End of the Tunnel

Some years ago I went with a group of Christian leaders from England to Israel-Palestine. One morning we sat in a hotel garden in East Jerusalem and listened to horror stories of oppression and cruelty imposed by Israelis on Palestinians. In the afternoon we sat in the Foreign Ministry in Jerusalem and heard horror stories of the loss suffered by Israelis at the hands of Palestinian suicide bombers. Where everyone is a victim and a hierarchy of victimhood becomes everyone's motivation, how do you seek reconciliation and where do you look for signs of hope? The then Deputy Foreign Minister was a rabbi by the name of Michael Melchior. He responded to our tough questioning with a remark that struck me then and that has not left me since. He said that sometimes it seems as if there is no light at the end of the tunnel. But it is not because the light is not there; it is because the tunnel is not straight.

We cannot know the future; we can only travel in hope and with faith. We will only be able to judge our lives from the end backwards. History can neither be written in advance, nor established contemporaneously with the living of it. But, we can recognise that change happens and that we change as we go and grow. In recognising that some of us have made decisions and choices that have created a good history as seen from the perspective of tomorrow, others have not. But it might make us a little more understanding of the latter because we come to comprehend the precariousness of the changing lives we lead as changing people in a changing world.

I am with Bob Dylan and Bono on this one. In *The Times They Are A-Changin'*, Dylan advises caution as the wheel is still turning, and the caution is wise. Be silent before judging yourself or other people: their journey is not complete yet. There is more to come. We will find what we are looking for, but it won't be in this life.

Chapter 6

GRACELAND

Not only do I remember where I was when the news of John F. Kennedy's assassination came through (I was 6 years old, had just had a bath and was sent early to bed by my parents and visiting grandparents when the news came over the small black and white television in the corner of the lounge), but also I remember exactly where I was the day Elvis Presley died.

I had finished my first year of language study at university and was spending some time in Austria meeting people who are still good friends today. I went into Linz in the early morning when the River Danube had flooded parts of the city and a newspaper billboard said 'Der König ist tot!' ('the King is dead!'). I puzzled for a little while because Austria does not have a monarchy, before realising that it was talking about someone else entirely. Elvis was dead and the circumstances were unpleasant.

When Elvis Presley died on 16 August 1977, the man who had revolutionised white music and had come to characterise the new pop stardom was no more. Bizarrely, a huge number of people still seem to think his death was faked and expect him to walk through the door any moment. Oh, and there are even people who worship him in the church that bears his name. Apart from these oddities, the rest of the world knows that Elvis will not be 're-entering the building'.

Elvis was buried at his home in Memphis, Tennessee. Graceland is now the subject of further development in order to milk money from the hundreds of thousands of tourists who visit the mansion and its estate every year. But, for many people it is also a place of almost religious devotion. The death of someone like Elvis (Princess Diana was similar in this respect) seems to destabilise a worryingly large number of people to the extent that they see him as some sort of a demigod who can't possibly have gone away and who can still mediate spiritual life and energy. Apart from its shameless (and, possibly, naïve) celebration of tacky wealth, raging success, human vulnerability, and its almost sentimental religious backdrop, Graceland has become not only a kitschy tourist attraction; it has also become a place of pilgrimage.

In 1986 Paul Simon recorded his *Graceland* album, thus bringing African rhythms to those of us who had never really come across them before. It seems hard to believe now, but what was later to become known as 'world music' was confined to a few enthusiasts who knew about such things. The only two other African musicians I had heard of were Hugh Masekela (the great trumpeter) and Miriam Makeba. Both influenced Paul Simon when he went to South Africa in 1985 seeking inspiration from African indigenous music. He recorded most of *Graceland* in Johannesburg, bringing to a new western audience not only songs influenced by South African dance music (including a cappella, isicathamiya and mbaqanga), but musicians whose names would thereafter become world famous – particularly Ladysmith Black Mambazo.

The album was followed by the powerful and moving *African Concert*, recorded live in Harare, Zimbabwe, with Makeba and other great musicians performing with stature and pride. Simon got into trouble with the United Nations and the ANC for breaking the boycott of South Africa over its apartheid regime, but the album and concert brought some hitherto obscure musicians to a global audience. It is impossible not to be moved by the final a cappella rendition by the whole stadium of the African anthem, 'Nkosi Sikele Africa' (God Bless Africa).

Well, maybe I have a rotten memory and everyone else in the UK already loved the music coming from the southern hemisphere; but I remember listening to the opening track, 'The Boy in the Bubble', and being hooked. The fusion of western rock with African rhythms was mesmerising. It made me want to dance – which is worrying, if you have ever seen me dance. 'Graceland' is the second track on the album and speaks of loss and uncertainty and pilgrimage and a journeying hope. Yet, it is also wonderfully ambiguous.

It is all too easy to look sneeringly at stars like Elvis who have fame and fortune, but whose lives appear later to betray loneliness, tragedy and self-doubt. In the United Kingdom, the media love to build people up before knocking them down and displaying their foibles and failures to a salacious world. It sometimes feels like a human being, with all his or her flaws, is just thrown into the middle of the arena where we can all enjoy their public humiliation and torture. They are dehumanised and turned into a commodity that can be bought and sold for the prurient titillation of a drooling public which loves to see the mighty fall. It is a scandal and a shame that millions of people buy the sort of cheap 'news'papers every day that are obsessed with 'celebrity' and feed this miserable trade in human frailty. Elvis was a supremely talented man who allowed himself to be manipulated by people he trusted; his death was miserable and lonely and far too early.

But, for all the ambiguities, contradictions and inconsistencies of his life, Elvis had at least grasped one thing of real importance: despite the messes we make and what Bruce Cockburn calls the 'angel/beast' nature of humanity, ('Burden of the Angel/Beast', *Dart to the Heart*, 1994) there is always the trace of a God of grace in the background offering hope where hope seems dim. Elvis sang about grace, knowing that it is a gift and never something to be earned or claimed as of right. God can neither be tamed nor bought and the recognition that his grasp of us is more important than our grasp of him is sometimes all we are left with when our lives fall apart. No wonder Elvis called his home 'Graceland'.

Paul Simon hints at this when he sings of the journey to Graceland being like a pilgrimage in the hope of finding not rejection, but welcome in the place of grace and generosity.

A Land of Grace?

I have listened to that song thousands of times and I never grow bored of it. But this is partly because it repeatedly makes me ask a question that won't let me go: what would a 'land of grace' look like? What would it be like to live somehow or somewhere where life is characterised by generosity and not by vindictiveness or constant judgement? I think there is an answer to this question and it invariably takes me back to a place simultaneously of familiarity and of a certain incredulity.

The New Testament gospels are full of encounters that ordinary people had with Jesus of Nazareth. This carpenter from the northern hills of Galilee had made his name by offending the religious establishment with words and deeds that seemed irreligious and even blasphemous. He mixed with the wrong people and transgressed social etiquette. Whereas the serious religious professionals ended up nailing him to a cross, it was those who had been told they were not welcome at God's table who found in Jesus an embrace of accepting love and generosity. I will try to illustrate this by showing how two of the gospels are supposed to work if we read them correctly. This will need a bit of explanation, but it is worth the effort.

Mark wrote the shortest gospel and did so with the worst Greek (although that hardly matters for our purposes). He shows little interest in great long theological discourses and goes straight for the action. After a brief introduction he has Jesus returning to Galilee 'proclaiming the good news of God' (Mark 1:14). Now, I am less interested in what we think this 'good news' should be and more interested in what would have been *heard* as 'good news' by the people of Galilee. In short, the only message that would have been heard as 'good news' was: 'the Romans are going'. Only when the Roman occupation ended and the Jews were free again in their own land to worship in their way would their history be vindicated, their identity affirmed and their God evidently present among them again. If you had asked them how they would recognise the coming of God among them again, they would have said: 'When we see the Romans leaving, then we will know God is with us.'

There is always a problem with human beings who see the world and God in a very particular way and insist that everybody else should see as they do – or be excluded from their 'believing' community. It was no different for the people of Jesus's time in his home region. In the first recorded words of his public ministry, Jesus spells out what is the 'good news of God' (Mark 1:14–15); but the problem is that it doesn't look like the expulsion of the Romans is included in it. This means that some people will not 'get it'. 'The time is fulfilled, the kingdom of God has come near. Repent and believe the good news', says Jesus. But what does he mean?

When he says that 'the time is fulfilled', people will immediately hear a message of imminent release from their 'exile' – their subjugation by the Roman Empire's guardians. If now is the time that we have been waiting for – the *kairos* of God – then we must look for the evidence: so, where is the rebellion starting and who is leading it? Jesus goes on: 'the kingdom of God has come near'. In other words, the presence of God is among us again and the time of our release and vindication is here at last; so, where do we see the evidence for this (the expulsion of the Roman/pagan oppressors)? Then Jesus makes the most arresting, challenging and disturbing demand: 'Repent!' But he doesn't mean what we usually assume he means when he uses this rather old-fashioned and seemingly negative word.

If you go out on the street in an English town and tell people to 'repent', they will either avoid you or call an ambulance from the local mental hospital. The word is understood to be a demand from miserable religious fundamentalists that everyone else should recognise their horribleness before God and become like them in their belief and life. But 'repentance' does not mean anything like this – especially in this context. The word comes from the Greek 'metanoia' which means literally 'change your mind'. Therefore, Jesus is inviting his hearers to change the way they look for the presence of God in order that they can see God differently, think about God (and the world and themselves) differently and, accordingly, live differently. The challenging question is: can you dare to see the presence of God while the Romans remain and your suffering continues (and may get considerably worse) – can you dare to see the presence of God in me (Jesus) while your circumstances remain grim or can you only recognise the presence of God in the way you have always thought you must? Literally, Jesus is asking them to radically change the way they think, daring to tick a different box when it comes to thinking about God and recognising his presence.

This 'conversion' can be described as a gradual reshaping of the 'lens behind the eyes' through which we (usually) unconsciously and unquestioningly see and understand life and its meaning – or lack of it. It is a process rather than a simple event.

When Jesus then goes on to say, 'believe in the good news', he is not saying what we in the contemporary western world generally take him to mean – that is, 'give intellectual assent to a set of propositions' – but inviting his hearers to commit themselves in body, mind and spirit to what they now see when they look through their reshaped 'lens'.

So, the message of Jesus (according to Mark) could be summed up as: God is among you, but not as you expected; he is present in me. Can you look differently in order to see differently in order to think differently in order to live differently? Can you see that the presence of God is here – even while you suffer under Roman oppression – and now live accordingly? The rest of the gospel of Mark answers these questions: some people could dare to see God in surprising ways, but some could not. Those who could not, who insisted that God could only be detected in a very particular way, sent Jesus to a gallows.

The fourth gospel (John) works similarly, but differently. John introduces his treatment with a theological reflection – a prologue.

> In the beginning was the Word, and the Word was
>   with God, and the Word was God.
> He was with God in the beginning.
> Through him all things were made; without him
>   nothing was made that has been made.
> In him was life, and that life was the light of men.
> The light shines in the darkness, but the darkness has
>   not understood it ... (John 1:1–5)

Then leap ahead to verse 14 and we read: 'The Word became flesh and made his dwelling among us. We have seen his glory, the glory of the One and Only, who came from the Father, full of grace and truth.' The rest of the gospel answers the question we are supposed to ask of verse 14: well, what did you see? If you have seen 'his glory' (his presence), what did it look like?

104

The answer given by both gospel writers (and Matthew and Luke also) is that some people recognised the presence/glory of God in Jesus of Nazareth and others did not. Those who did tended to be people who had no status, no claims on public or religious reputation, no credibility in 'normal' society. Women, 'unclean' people, the rejected and marginalised found in Jesus a clear reflection of the character of God and responded accordingly; the religiously committed people (men) saw that Jesus didn't tick the right religious boxes and, therefore, couldn't possibly be anything other than a charlatan or a nuisance.

The point of this is that the gospels show us – illustrate in flesh-and-blood encounters – what it is to open ourselves to the possibility of receiving God's generosity. 'Grace-land' looks like a place characterised by people finding themselves to have been found by God and liberated to live a new life – regardless of the suffering and oppression of their actual circumstances or the opinions of those who claim to speak for God. 'Grace-land' is that place where a woman caught in the act of adultery finds her humiliation challenged and a new start possible; it is the place where a man who is stigmatised by an infectious illness finds himself drawn back into society and given a new life; it is the place where Jesus challenges the religiosity of those who think God is more interested in keeping to his rules than actually being generous to desperate people. It is significant that when Jesus heals someone before an audience of clergy, they don't throw a party to celebrate the presence and love of God; instead, they damn him because he did it on the wrong day (the Sabbath). They had forgotten what the 'rules' were supposed to be for:

a means to an end, the end being the reception of God's grace and mercy.

Mike Riddell once wrote a wonderful little book called *Godzone* (Lion, 1992). That was his word for what the gospel writers call variously 'the Kingdom of God' and 'the Kingdom of heaven', and Elvis Presley calls 'Graceland'. It is the place where we no longer have to hide behind pretensions of success or achievement, of self-righteousness or self-justification, because we know ourselves to be in need and we no longer feel the compulsion to pretend. When Adam and Eve sinned in the Garden of Eden and got found out by God who went looking for them (not the other way round, note), they realised they were 'naked' – transparent. They could be seen through and they were embarrassed and fearful. When 'lost' people met Jesus, they saw that they had been seen through, but found the experience liberating and renewing. Being exposed by and before God ceased to be threatening and became the source of a new freedom. That is Graceland.

Just to wrap this thread up, the logic of the Bible could be set out like this: if you want to know what God is like, look at Jesus; if you want to know what Jesus is like, read the gospels and (this is the scary bit) look at us, those who bear his name. The Church is supposed to be that community of graced people who reflect to the world what we see of Jesus in the gospels. In other words, when people touch, hear or see Christian communities, they should recognise in their life, speech, touch, priorities and relationships something of what they read of Jesus in the gospels. That is surely what it means to be 'the body' of Christ. We will come back to this in a later chapter.

A reason to believe ...

This notion actually takes us back even further. Paul Simon isn't the only one who needs to know why he is on the journey to Graceland in his song. All of us need to know why we believe what we believe and why it matters.

I explained in an earlier chapter how I grew up in a Christian home in Liverpool and never really knew anything other than belonging to a Christian community where people genuinely cared for each other and knew that they had been found by the God who still 'walks in the garden in the cool of the day asking: "Adam, where are you?"' (Genesis 3:8–9). But growing up and away from the support of that community left me more isolated and for the first time asking some scary fundamental questions about God, meaning and integrity. I needed to know (as an adult) that Christianity is true, not just if it 'works for me'. The content of the faith had to be credible and robust or we all risk wasting our time being credulous victims of a psychological fraud. 'Belief' is not the same as credulity and 'faith' is not, as one 6-year-old put it, 'believing in things you know aren't true'. Believing involves reason and belief must be reasonable.

But this is not a quick journey whose destination is reached after a swift five-minute think. In my experience so far I would say it involves a lifetime of thinking, rethinking, doubting, questioning, affirming, celebrating and worrying. But that is also the exciting thing about Christian faith: you don't just 'arrive' one day and then bask in the glory of universal wisdom; rather, you go on a very long journey of working it all out, of (in the word Jesus used) 'repenting'. Indeed, it seems to me that 'conversion' involves the lifelong process of having the lens behind the eyes reshaped so that, having had our eyes opened to the possibility of a new way of seeing God, the world and us, we increasingly begin to see more clearly, as God sees. Anyone who engages the brain at all knows that life is full of surprises, that the road we travel is full of twists and turns, that the light changes as the day moves on and the familiar scene suddenly looks different.

This is why Christian hope is rooted not in some grand schema worked out to our convenience, or in a timetable for the end of the world, but in a person – the person and character of God. You don't have to look very far to find people who have a fixed view of God and the way he works and then pin their faith on a particular series of events taking place. For example, the person who loses all trust in God because they get cancer or their relationship falls apart. Or the person who has unwittingly turned God into the genie whose job it is to make life comfortable and secure. Or the charlatans who promise that if you get the 'God' formula right (which usually involves giving huge amounts of money to them), God will reward you with health and wealth. The implications of this last one are serious and the pastoral fall-out is often painful to witness: it implies that if you are not successful and not healthy, it is because (a) there is something wrong with you, (b) you have sinned or (c) God probably has it in for you. This is iniquitous as well as pastorally or theologically indefensible.

GRACELAND

The Hopeful Story

It might be helpful if I sketch out the essential Christian story as this appears in the Bible. In doing so, we have to remember that if the Bible is the 'Word of God', it is only a means to point us to the 'end' which is the 'Word made flesh' who is the 'image' of the living God. That's the logic of Scripture and it can be summed up as: it is all about God and whether or not he is trustworthy. The story might look something like this (although this involves a couple of large leaps and the omission of a few details):

> In the beginning God created all that is. He called a particular people to show the diverse peoples of the world who he is and what he (his character) is about. This people took its 'chosenness' as privilege (we have been chosen, therefore we must be special, and the world should recognise our specialness) instead of responsibility to lay down their life that the world might see what God is like. The prophets came along and warned them that if they did not recover their original vocation (to enable the world to see what God is like), they would lose everything that spoke of their history, identity and vocation. Indeed, that is precisely what happened and the people went into exile twice, in the eighth and sixth centuries BC. Jesus fulfilled in himself what was always the calling of Israel and gave his life that the world might know what God is about. He then called the people who bear his name to live out in their world what was fulfilled in him – which was what had always been the vocation of his people: to show the world who he is and what he is about. The future is in God's hands and we are to just get on with being the body of Christ now.

109

This means that evangelism is really doing what Jesus was doing in Mark 1:14–15 and inviting people to see God and to see God differently – and then introducing them to a community of people who have dared to do this themselves and are now committed to enabling others to see what God is like and on whose side God is to be found. In other words, the job of the Christian Church is to be a community in which the grace, mercy, reconciling and healing love of God are to be found. And this is what people should encounter and call 'Grace-land'.

However, some will say that the Church has obviously missed the point somewhere along the line because the Christian community is not always seen as a place of mercy where God is to be found and reflected. Well, I will put my hands up straight away and cry 'mea culpa'. As someone once said, the Church often seems to be more a reminder of the bad news than a proclaimer of the good news of God in Christ. That, again, is indisputably true. But, like many institutions in today's world, the British national media representation of the Church is generally negative and extremely selective, while local experience is more positive. While recognising that this isn't necessarily true of other countries, I will illustrate from a British perspective.

The Church of England is organised territorially. That is to say, it covers every inch of England and everyone who lives anywhere in England lives in an Anglican parish. A parish priest is not merely the chaplain of his or her church, but the vicar of all the people who live or work in the parish. This brings not only legal responsibilities and a general availability to all who live there, but also an inevitable commitment to the well-being of that whole community and a missionary perspective to all ministry (meaning an outward-looking reaching towards those in the parish who have neither heard nor encountered the 'good news' of God).

Being a bishop in the Church of England brings with it the massive privilege of seeing the reality of daily life in and through our parishes and the amazing commitment of clergy and lay people to their ministry and outreach. Many parish churches stand at the heart of a community and offer not just 'spiritual' sustenance and worship, but also facilities for all sorts of people at all sorts of stages of life. Groups for asylum seekers, children, young people, refugees, young parents, elderly people, etc. are to be found all over the country. When the Church gets a bad press – usually based on prejudice rather than reality – this massive local commitment to the wellbeing of others is ignored. Millions of hours of voluntary work are given through our churches every week and the basis of this commitment is simply this: if God's grace has been received, it has to be passed on.

Now, this is not to excuse the bad examples of churches going wrong and being a 'reminder of the bad news'. There are always examples of Christians who speak and act in ways that do not reflect the priorities of Jesus as we read them in the gospels. You don't have to scratch too deeply to find inconsistencies, contradictions, weaknesses and failures on the part of Christians like me, or their churches. But this should not be a surprise. The Church does not claim to be the locus of totally consistent behaviour and a complete appropriation of 'truth'. We are still human, still learning, still incomplete in our understanding and still manage to get it wrong a million times. But the 'lens' is still in the process of being reshaped and our journey with Jesus and his friends continues.

One of the remarkable things about the gospels is the way they describe the followers of Jesus. These were ordinary people who found *as they journeyed with Jesus* that they were beginning to catch a glimpse of God being present among them in the way Jesus had suggested. The change of theological worldview was radical and it took time. Yet Jesus never once despised his friends for their limited vision, their moral failures or over-inflated self-understanding. Rather, he gave them the space and the time to look and watch and see and touch and think and express their sillynesses – all without being cast out from among the group. Their internal disputes and power-struggles were addressed as they occurred, but Jesus seemed in no hurry to demand perfection from them instantly. Follow the story of Simon Peter through the gospels and into the book called The Acts of the Apostles and you see the inconsistencies and character flaws continuing beyond resurrection and even Pentecost.

All this should help us to realise that 'Grace-land' – the community where this Jesus is followed – is a place of realism, not fantasy. It is where people find that they can escape the judgement of the world 'out there' that is so unforgiving and loves to trap people in the reputation of the past, and find a new start. This is a community of grace and generosity where belonging is not conditional on conformity, and where perfection is not demanded even before the 'journey' has begun. In this sense Christian discipleship is about meeting Jesus, imitating Jesus, learning to be forgiving as well as forgiven, and then putting up with the messiness of our co-disciples as we try together to reflect in our life together the face and touch and voice of the Jesus we read about in the gospels.

I am not sure what Paul Simon really hoped to find when he got to Memphis, Tennessee. He indicates that he hoped to find that 'we all will be received in Graceland'. I cannot for the life of me see that anyone could wish for anything else. I don't think there is much hope to be found in a dead rock 'n' roll singer whose grave has become a tourist attraction as well as a shrine, but hope is to be found in the grace that Elvis knew to be the character of the God as seen in Jesus of Nazareth.

Chapter 7

I STILL HAVEN'T FOUND
WHAT I'M LOOKING FOR

I remember very vividly the night the penny dropped and I decided to be a follower of Jesus. I was 11 years old and had been brought up in a very large Sunday School at Richmond Baptist Church in Anfield, Liverpool. I moved from primary to secondary school and found myself in an environment that was – how can I put it? – more 'challenging' than the benign milieu of the much smaller school I had known since I started at the age of four. The Holt Comprehensive School in Childwall, Liverpool, brought in students from a variety of areas and backgrounds and I found myself to be in a very small minority of those who went to church. My own weekly routines involved the youth group, the youth club, Sunday services, Bible study groups and belonging with older teenagers who seemed to have their lives mapped out before them. This experience was alien to many of my new friends and it had a bizarre effect on me. I now write with the benefit of hindsight and wider experience, but I look back with some embarrassment as well as understanding about why I was the way I was during those school years.

The Religious Education teacher was a man we knew as 'Moses'. He was a committed Christian who saw

115

the seriousness of young people in a comprehensive school being taught well about religion in general and Christianity in particular. He also knew he could not start any form of Christian group in the school as it would have little credibility, coming from an RE teacher. But he did take the risk of inviting three or four of us to a meeting of some inter-school Christian Union one evening at the YMCA in Mount Pleasant in Liverpool city centre. I remember feeling sick all the way there because of his driving. I also remember being bored all evening and wondering where all these young teenagers had come from. And I remember being unimpressed by the speaker, a Church Army youth evangelist. But at the end of his unmemorable talk he offered a copy of John's gospel to anyone who wanted to take Jesus seriously and I thought I would at least go home with the freebie.

When I got home that evening, 10 October 1969, I went up to the bedroom I shared with my younger brother and started to read this gospel. Something clicked. I seemed to grasp for the first time what it meant to choose to become a follower of Jesus – a Christian. I knelt by my bed and, with all the limitations of an 11-year-old and all the seriousness of an adult, asked God to make me a disciple of Jesus, to help me to live for him as he forgave me my sins and set me on a new course in life. Don't ask me how, but when I stood up I knew I was now on a different road; and although I couldn't see even beyond the first bend, I knew something had changed and my orientation in life was not geared towards simply fulfilling myself.

Despite my ignorance of the wider universe and the extents of human experience at that point, I did think that something significant had happened to me. I now look back and think that this was both infinitely good (discovering the reality of God so early and trying thereafter to live a life that was not self-obsessed) and sadly bad (preoccupation with 'getting it right', fear of the consequences of sinning and a compulsive need to rescue other people from eternal damnation). My teenage years saw me running a Christian group at this comprehensive school and getting a lot of embarrassing humiliation for doing so, never quite being 'in' any group of friends at school and taking life far too seriously. I think I viewed God more sternly than he viewed me, but it would take a long time for me to work this out.

I left school and went to study German and French at the University of Bradford where the language courses concentrated on language (translation and interpreting) rather than literature, and politics rather than 'high culture'. I loved the study, although I was never a natural linguist like some of my fellow students. I lacked the confidence of some of my friends and discovered that in comparison with them I was a rather inexperienced human being. What I did have, however, was a sense that life had to be worth more than consuming huge amounts of alcohol, proving the power of your libido and ignoring the wider world. The study of politics (particularly German history and political development) opened my eyes to the complexity of historical evolution and the almost serendipitous nature of what politicians often pretend is intentional decision/action. For me, the world became bigger, less monochrome and harder to understand. And in all this, of course, my theology was finding itself challenged to the roots.

I belonged to the Christian Union at Bradford and was active in my first year and a half in evangelism among other students. I now look back on those years and wish I had had the courage to be honest about what was going on inside me and face some of the tough questions openly instead of internalising them intellectually and emotionally. But the student Christian community was a place for certainties, not questions, for orthodoxy and not curiosity. What partly kept me sane during this time was the welcoming and non-judgemental Anglican church I had begun to attend with some friends. This church gave me space and combined real pastoral care with allowing me the freedom to be myself. Surprisingly, this was a little threatening because I didn't know how to cope with a questioning environment such as this that took worship seriously, yet seemed to recognise the humanity of Christians like me. The vicar didn't seem to worry too much about not having everything wrapped up. And it was his humanity rather than his spirituality that kept me hanging on.

I spent the subsequent couple of years working in Austria (with a church youth group), Germany (as a freelance technical translator near Stuttgart) and France (with a telecommunications company in Paris). I have described elsewhere the challenges to my faith while I was in Germany and I still think of this time as one of the most important periods of my life – though also one of the most uncomfortable. This experience of isolation cut through the slender threads of religious fear and forced me to face the hard questions, not only intellectually, but existentially. The course this set me upon still continues to this day.

Linda and I got married after we had graduated (she did a degree in nursing at the University of Manchester) and we moved to Cheltenham immediately after our honeymoon. I soon began retraining in Russian at the Government Communications Headquarters and subsequently worked as a linguist specialist in the closed world behind the barbed-wire fences at Oakley. We eventually joined an Anglican-Methodist Church in the town centre and helped run the youth work there. Yet during all this time I was feeling my way theologically and as a human being, learning to be a husband and father and so on. Life through the church could not (in my experience) be divorced from the work I was doing during the week and the way I was confronted by an immensely complex, ambiguous and often dirty world of subterfuge, cruelty, power mongering and military violence. The experience at GCHQ shaped my understanding of the world to such an extent that I became increasingly frustrated with simplistic theological formulae that could only emanate from a naïve apprehension or experience of the world.

I indicated earlier how this made my time at theological college somewhat frustrating. We went to Bristol for three years in 1984 as I had been selected for training for ordained ministry in the Church of England. The emphasis (by students, not the academic staff) there on 'my ministry', 'my gifts', 'my God' sat increasingly uncomfortably with the world I had emerged from, but was not allowed to speak about. I found it hard to make the connections between the theology we seemed to be developing and the reality of the world I had experienced through my work. I realise that this frustration says more about me and my limitations than it does about my fellow ordinands and other members of the college community. But it also raises questions about the engagement of theology with a more complex world than is sometimes posited in such institutions. The world is not tidy, and theology should neither be squeezed to fit the world as we would like to see it, nor made the preserve of a narcissistic spirituality that might satisfy individuals but fails to take seriously the messiness of the world 'out there'.

The point of labouring this story (while leaving out a huge amount of detail of the twists and turns of events) is to emphasise that I did not become a Christian and spend the rest of my life on an upward trajectory to a certain heaven. I did not arrive at a completed worldview that now only has to be massaged until I die. I actually started a life journey that has never stopped being challenging and surprising. Just as for the early followers of Jesus in the gospels, the walk with Jesus is not to be undertaken by people who want a quiet life in which their prejudices about God and the world are reinforced (usually in their own favour); it is a journey of surprise, challenge, awakening and growing exposure to all that life can throw at us – and all the while learning that God is present *in* all the ambiguities and inconsistencies and sufferings, not exempting us from them or keeping us 'clean' from them.

A BBC presenter once asked me on 'live' radio how I had managed to go from being 'a spy to a vicar'. I responded by saying that there is only one world and that God has to engage with the complexities of that world, or he is not God. Theology has to make sense of the real world and not be a self-contained set of self-evidently 'true' propositions that only relate to where life happens to be reasonably OK. The world is complicated and messy, but human beings are the same whether you are dealing with military machinations during the Cold War or individuals in a rural community in northern England. Scratch any human being and you find they bleed the same blood as the rest of us. Strip off the veneer of self-sufficiency or pride from an Indonesian peasant or a financial genius in New York and you find the same insecurities, fears and hopes, albeit expressed in different ways. It might sound stupidly obvious, but every human being is mortal and this recognition shapes how we live. I also added that if God (or my theology) cannot cope with the muckiness of real life, then he isn't worth acknowledging, let alone following.

This means also that a proper critical engagement with difficult issues can only be done by Christians who have their brains engaged (and can live with the tensions of not knowing everything) and the curiosity to explore the world God has put us in. I think it is artists who are often the people who expose the tensions and honestly explore the realities of living in a complicated world.

I sort of grew up with U2, but began with their second album. The youthful *October* (1981) set the scene for what was to follow. Songs of spiritual recognition and searching (*Gloria*, or *Tomorrow*, for example) mingle with the exploration of love and lust. The passionate expression of frustration with the grief of the Irish conflict finds its way through the music and lyrics, driving the audience to feel with the band that what they are singing about really matters. As the albums rolled off, so the concern for the world and politics grew

121

and developed – anger at injustice raging through an appreciation and celebration of the beauty of the world and life within it.

It was *The Joshua Tree* (1987) that really sealed U2's success and led to them being branded 'the biggest band in the world'. Many Christians in the UK who had followed U2's progress and loved the fact that the band members were open about their Christian commitment (having met in a church group in Ireland) now began to worry. Bono seemed to be going off the boil a bit and asking questions he shouldn't. What's worse, he even made a big hit out of a song that seems to say that being a Christian is not the all-satisfying end of the human journey: *I Still Haven't Found What I'm Looking For*.

But for many others, this was a moment of liberation as verbal expression was given to what most Christians know, but don't always articulate: that being a Christian does not fulfil every aspect of human experience after all. It renders ridiculous the notion (often expressed) that Jesus meets all our needs and makes us complete – try saying that to someone who is desperate for the touch and physical affection of another human being or someone trapped in the most isolating, debilitating and destructive depression.

I am with Bono on this one. I think he has read his gospels and understood what following Jesus is really all about. And his conclusion that 'knowing Jesus' is not the panacea for all the world's ills and doesn't ensure every individual's existential well-being is surely accurate. What I can't quite understand is why it took a song by an Irish rock band to make me identify what I actually felt about being a Christian in a complicated world. The annoying thing is that any reading of the

Bible demonstrates clearly that faithful following of God often leads to trouble: consider Abraham, Moses, David, Jeremiah, Mary, Peter, Paul and so on. Jesus himself promised that anyone who followed him should not expect anything other than to carry a cross (and, presumably, get nailed to it). Faithful discipleship has never led inevitably to some sort of painless utopia where the less pleasant realities of life simply pass you by.

My own experience is that I follow Jesus because I believe he is the one who leads us to God; I will follow him into an engagement with the world that reflects his own coming *into* the material world and not exempting himself from it. I expect no spiritual rewards for this and will continue to follow him even if I feel nothing and gain nothing but trouble. Why? Because I believe that the truth about God, the world and us is to be found in him.

But that doesn't mean that he fills every niche of my being. He doesn't make me feel better when I am ill, or happier when I am sad, or fitter when I am lazy. He doesn't exist in order to make life more comfortable for me or anyone else. He is not the god of the comfort gaps. Knowing Jesus means seeing God and the world through his eyes and then trying to live accordingly – whatever the cost. It means believing in and trusting the God who raised Jesus from the dead and not worrying too much about the rest of it all.

Now, this can sound a bit odd, especially coming from a bishop. But it is true. Yes, putting my faith in the God who raised Jesus from the dead means that life (how I see it, understand it and live it) is transformed: I know I am forgiven and can forgive – so, relationships should be transformed by my being a Christian and living a Christ-like life. Indeed, I will live differently and, hopefully, attract others to do similarly – and this will change the way we live together in any society. Living the way Jesus expects his followers to live will challenge the superficiality of the world out there and will transform people's lives. But none of this will guarantee happier feelings, greater success in business, a larger bank balance or a more comfortable life. As Jesus once said (and we observed earlier), the only promise is a cross. You live a Christian life in order to give it away, to lose it.

There are a number of stories in the gospels that seem to make this point in a very suggestive way. In the 'Parable of the Talents' (Matthew 25:14–30) a man gives money to his servants before he leaves on a business trip. Each of the three servants receives an amount according to his ability to do something with it. When the man returns from his travels he finds that two servants have doubled their money and he commends them for their work. The third, who was given the smallest amount (that is, less to have to worry about losing), had gone off, dug a hole in the ground and buried the money where it couldn't be harmed. The business man was furious when he found out: the servant could at the very least have invested the money or loaned it on interest!

The point seems to be that Jesus is talking about his friends being reckless enough to throw the gospel (the good news of God) out there into the big, wide and mucky world and see what happens. The gospel is not to be wrapped up and hidden in order to preserve it in its original form. Throwing it 'out there' means risking it getting stolen, lost, abused, hijacked, distorted and ignored. But Jesus seems to be telling his friends to take the risk and be commended for it; not to make the mistake of thinking that God's primary preoccupation is guaranteeing that his people preserve this gospel in its original pristine condition. Of course, risking losing it is dangerous; but that seems to be what Jesus is asking his friends to do. (Which then begs the question of why some in the Church are so obsessed with preserving what they deem to be the 'immutable' bits that they spend time, money and energy in fighting those who want to dig the 'talent' out of the ground and expose it to some real life danger.)

In the 'Parable of the Mustard Seed' (Matthew 13:31–32; Mark 4:30–32) Jesus seems equally reckless. The tiny mustard seed is planted and eventually grows into a large tree. That bit is fine and we can be happy with the image that the kingdom of God grows from tiny beginnings into something wonderfully fruitful. But Jesus adds a detail that spoils the contentment of the complacent: the birds of the air can apparently make their nests in the branches of this tree. And what is so bad about that, you ask? Well, the tree doesn't get to choose which birds will make their nests in which particular branches. And this is hopelessly untidy because the 'wrong' birds might take advantage of this sloppy openness and make their grubby nests where we don't want them. In other words, once you have planted the 'gospel' or the 'kingdom of God', you lose control over it and have to learn to watch all sorts of messy things being done with it.

Two other parables ram this point home in a subtle way. The 'Sower' sows his seed and it falls on four types of ground. Some grows and some doesn't. Many preachers seem to explain this parable by concentrating on the types of ground (getting your evangelism right and not wasting resources) or the nature of the seed (what *is* the Word of God?). But this misses the obvious point – that the story is meant to be about the bloke who sows the seed and the manner in which he does it: he chucks it around everywhere and seems utterly wasteful. He doesn't carefully plant one seed where he knows it will grow and then water it every day – thus getting a 100 per cent return on his investment. Rather, he throws it out in the most wasteful, extravagant and profligate way and doesn't seem to worry about whether some of it gets lost, misused or trodden into the ground.

Jesus also speaks of wheat growing in a field. The farmer's enemy comes along and plants weeds among the wheat (Matthew 13:24–30). When the workers ask if they should go through the field and weed out the rubbish, the owner refuses to let them – on the grounds that to do so will risk uprooting the good wheat as well. So, says the owner, just let it all grow together and we'll sort it all out at the end. Or, in relation to the good news, the gospel, don't worry so much about the messiness and risk to its 'purity' – just get it out there and let it grow. God can worry about sorting it all out later.

These are just a sample of the perspectives Jesus gives us on how to handle our faith in God and the good news of God's presence in Jesus of Nazareth. He seems to be less concerned than many Christians about being defended or about the lengths we sometimes go to in trying to protect the faith from being messed up by its exposure to the realities of the big wide world. No wonder they crucified him.

And this brief excursion through a few parables brings us back to the matter of the world's complexity and the fact that Christians do not – by virtue of their faith – have the ultimate insight into every human question, nor the ultimate panacea to every existential challenge. On the contrary, Christians are people who acknowledge at every turn that they are 'sinners' who fail to see as God sees and fail to reflect Jesus in the world. We have no problem recognising our inconsistencies and weaknesses. Indeed, we claim to be grasped by a God who is unsurprised by how we really are – a God who chose to come among us as one of us and share all the limitations of being a human being in a contingent world. Knowing that we do not know everything is not a problem. Facing challenges that have never existed before is something we do along with everyone else in the world. But we also know that God's coming among us as one of us sheds new light and hope on the whole process of living.

This leads me to say that if I have to make a choice between being in a 'pure' church or a 'messy' church, I will go with the latter. A messy church seems to me to fit better with what Jesus had in mind when he went about mixing with the 'wrong' people, sharing the good news of God with unlikely people in unlikely places, throwing it out there and seeing what happened. He also recognises that this world is not straightforward and has an infinite capacity for surprise and threat as well as hope and promise. This makes it inevitable that Christians will take different positions on many of the challenges that face the world in the twenty-first century and one or two of these can be used to illustrate the matter.

Climate change now dominates the political agenda in a way that would have been unimaginable only a decade ago. The industrialised world has found it impossible to avoid the challenge that its industry has generated: that the world is warming and that choices have to be made urgently if the future of our grandchildren's planet is to be secured. The matter is being taken seriously by many countries where the consumer demand has already provided wealth and technological facilities still dreamed of by the world's poorest people. And there lies the rub: the now-emerging countries of Asia and Africa are being asked to hold back their own economic and industrial development because it is so destructive of the atmosphere in terms of pollution of air and land. But these same countries rightly express some indignation that the countries that 'have' are not in a strong moral position when it comes to asking the 'weak' to sacrifice yet again. The industrialised countries colonised and exploited the countries that gave them their natural resources (and more) and now have the nerve to ask the same exploited people to forego their own turn.

This illustrates both how some problems only emerge in time and that history is not a tidy art. Christians hold to 'justice' as something every human being and every society should honour and respect. Justice can be said to demand that the newly developing countries should have the same opportunities the rest of us have. But the same concept of 'justice' also demands that a global sacrifice is made in deposing the god of consumer growth. How are these two needs to be reconciled? Clearly, there are those who just wish the whole matter would go away and leave us in peace to continue the way of the world as we know it. But this is not acceptable and we must argue the matter out in an informed and intelligent way that takes account of history, mutuality, sacrifice, science, ethics, poverty, power and theology.

Christians might well come down on different sides when it comes to proposing solutions and compromises. Some Christians, basing their judgements on similar theological and ethical criteria, will assume some elements of the debate to be of greater importance than others – and these might derive from their own personal experience, origins, background, etc. In other words, resolving such matters even within the community of Christians will not be easy because the world and its issues are complex, and human beings are limited in understanding, experience and the will to 'see differently' or change.

Climate change is just one obvious example, but I could illustrate the point with dozens of other issues. I engage in a global interfaith initiative based in Central Asia (Kazakhstan) which brings together world religious leaders, politicians and non-governmental organisations. We would need a separate book (at least) to even begin to explore some of the complexities of language, perception and politics involved in such conversations.

Bioethical debates in Britain and Europe are fraught with difficulty because of the different assumptions made by diverse parties to the conversations. It sometimes seems as though the technology has developed far faster than our ability to process the ethics of scientific development in some areas. Couple this with an instinctive reflex on the part of some religious leaders to pronounce in colourful language on complicated scientific processes, when it is obvious that they have not been well-informed and do not understand the science involved, and you have a media dream.

Then you have to set this against a philosophical backdrop in some parts of Europe according to which the 'secular humanist' worldview arrogantly claims the ground of 'neutrality', thereby placing 'religious' people somewhere up the 'loony' (irrational and dangerous) scale. This allows some scientists, journalists and commentators to see any critique from a religious perspective as problematic and deserving only of ridicule – without once having to question the philosophical assumptions and presuppositions that shape their own worldview. (It would certainly help, however, if religious leaders would vow only to speak when they have learned and understood what is *actually* being proposed in such instances as the creation of hybrid embryos in early 2008.)

Christians will come to different conclusions in respect of the desirability of such embryo research and will give different weight to different elements of the arguments. Some will do so out of fear, some out of irrational suspicion, others out of informed and intelligent research and argument. But in the end they will have to make a judgement and live with the fact that other equally committed Christians will come to a diametrically opposed conclusion. And Christians will also have to learn to resist intelligently the nonsense that allows commentators (in the UK, at least) to ridicule the worldviews of religious people while remaining ignorant of the unargued-for assumptions that they regard as self-evidently true and, therefore, neutral.

Still Looking

I guess this will all be very annoying to the sorts of Christians who want to believe that 'Jesus is the answer' before they have had to face the complexities of the 'question'. The world is messy and complicated and we do not do God or the faith a service by reducing everything to a simplistic slogan. Bono has grown up and honestly faced the reality that human beings are limited and cannot arrive in paradise in a mortal life in a contingent world. His curiosity and refusal to be satisfied seem to reflect what Jesus himself saw as the key to the kingdom of God: being like a child. Children are infinitely curious, persistent in asking questions, happy to live with fluid boundaries between different 'worlds', creative and optimistic, learning and changing.

Perhaps this is why Jesus referred to himself not as the 'destination', but as the 'way' (John 14:6) and why the first Christian communities were known as people of 'the Way' (Acts 9:2 and 24:14). By definition they have not completed their journey, but continue to muddle their way through 'Godzone', doing their best to live God's way, but ultimately leaving it to God to sort it all out when the end eventually comes.

I still haven't found what I'm looking for. I know that God has found me and that in Jesus a new world has begun. I am convinced that God-in-Christ is the best news the world has ever seen and heard. I would love everyone to find the freedom Jesus offers when we see God, the world and ourselves through his eyes and begin to live his way together. I have experienced so much of the new life and lifestyle God shows us in Jesus. But I am still curious, strangely unsatisfied, open to learn and experience more and not at all worried about irritating those whose fears make them want to wrap the faith up and keep it as a possession. I am happy to give it away, lose it, risk it and leave the rest to God who had the audacity to not be intimidated even by death.

Chapter 8

BRAND NEW DAY

I feel sorry for young people just emerging into a world of wonderful music and discovering the amazing Van Morrison. Many people know his songs without realising they are his: *Moondance* and *Brown-eyed Girl* are just two examples. But you'd have to have the stamina of a dinosaur to work your way through his prolific output which began in the 1960s and hasn't stopped yet.

The Irishman is legendary not only for his music, but also for his apparent misery. For someone who pens such beautiful, powerful and moving lyrics about the richness and often contradictory variety of human experience, he is remarkably short of words when it comes to any attempt to interview him. He is notorious for playing whole sets without addressing a single word to the audience. In one sense this is wonderful: he is a musician and people who go to his gigs want to hear him play, not pontificate about the world and its issues in mini-sermons. But some fans do wish he would communicate just something – anything – in between the songs.

I have a soft spot for Van Morrison for another reason. When I was a vicar in Rothley, Leicestershire (1992–2000), a friend of mine was a pilot who often flew famous people to famous places. One day he told me he was flying Van Morrison to a jazz festival in Molde, Norway. Never missing an opportunity, I asked him to see if the great man had any spare copies of his new album recorded at Ronnie Scott's jazz club in London with Georgie Fame only a few months before. (I had missed the two of them at Ronnie Scott's, but caught Georgie Fame performing on his own there the following week.) When Alan got back he popped a postcard of Molde through my door. On the back, in very spidery handwriting were the words: 'To Nick the Vic from Van the Man – rock on'. I gather he had had 'a little bit to drink' when he was helped to write it.

Brand New Day appears on the *Moondance* album from 1970, but it is a song I keep going back to. Like Bruce Cockburn's *All the Diamonds* it is a wonderfully simple and evocative celebration of the world we live in. It doesn't get onto any of Van Morrison's compilation or greatest hits albums and (in my experience) is not widely known, but I think it is up there with the best of his output. It is an expression of the sense of freedom and well-being you can get when a bright new day dawns and the sun shines and you feel strangely satisfied. Nothing too deep and nothing too fancy.

We will come back to Van Morrison's brand new day in a moment, but I want to digress for a little while and offer a different artistic contrast to the optimism of the enigmatic Irishman.

The Lives of Others (*Das Leben der Anderen*) was released in 2006 and went on to win the 'Best Film' award at the European Film Awards 2006, the 2007 Academy Award (Oscar) for 'Best Foreign Language

Film' and a nomination for Golden Globe in 2007. It is an intelligent, sensitive and moving German film (written and directed by Florian Henckel von Donnersmarck) about a Stasi (Staatssicherheit, State Security) officer in the old German Democratic Republic a few years before the fall of the Berlin Wall. The officer, Wiesler, is part of the brutal regime that imprisoned its population and tried to coerce loyalty from its subjects. The devoted Wiesler sets up surveillance on a playwright whose lover is wanted by the Minister of Culture. Political intrigue and human drama drive the film to a sad, touching and optimistic conclusion which celebrates the potential nobility of surprising people and recognises the fallibility of ordinary people who find themselves caught on the horns of terrible dilemmas.

Following the fall of the Berlin Wall in 1989 the worryingly voluminous files of the Stasi were opened up, revealing the extent of surveillance and corruption in the GDR during its relatively short existence as a country. Files had been kept on around six million people – one-third of the total population. Anyone suspected of any form of disloyalty could be spied upon and find their life ruined. It is reckoned that a quarter of the population were in some way compromised by the Stasi in informing on their family, friends, colleagues or neighbours. When the files were eventually made available people were horrified to discover who it was who had been informing on them and a new light was shed on past relationships.

The film illustrates brilliantly the drab, grey monotony of life behind the Iron Curtain. The playwright, Georg Dreyman, keeps on the right side of the authorities by writing dramas that extol the virtues of the proletariat and he is introduced in the film at the performance of a play set in a factory with workers dressed in grey uniforms. Such drama is not intended to explore the vast experiences and potential of human beings in a wonderful world, but simply to reinforce the ideological dogmas of the retarded pragmatists who 'ran' countries such as the GDR. A 'good' drama was one that towed the line of socialist orthodoxy regardless of the discrepancy between this and the aspirations of the people in its grip. *The Lives of Others* depicts a grey world filled with grey people doing grey things to people who long for some colour.

One of the saddest points made by the film is the high number of suicides among artists in the GDR. The State stopped recording the numbers of suicides in the late 1970s – presumably because these provided an inconvenient contradiction to the marvellous utopia that the GDR was supposed to be. The number of artists (in its broadest sense) who committed suicide during the GDR years was particularly high and the film suggests why this was the case. In one scene Wiesler has broken into Dreyman's apartment and removes a copy of something by Bertolt Brecht. Wiesler is shown reading this book with intense bewilderment. Everything in the scene – including Wiesler's uniform and hair – is grey ... apart from the cover of the book which is bright yellow. It is as if 'art' brings colour into the drabness of a cruel and inhuman polity.

The role of an artist is to explore the world and challenge our perceptions of it. The nature of the artist is to shine light into dark places and encourage us to see the world differently. Dramatists, poets and painters are free to break all the rules in order to open our eyes to a wider reality: think of Picasso and the infancy of cubism; or remember that Mozart's music was considered childish and whimsical by his contemporaries. So many artists took their own lives in the GDR and other eastern bloc countries during the latter half of the twentieth century because this natural instinct was forcibly suppressed. If you brought colour into the world, you were suspected of being pro-western. The philistines who tried to shape a socialist culture effectively sucked the blood out of those very people whose nature and vocation was to wonder at the world and splash its colour (including grey) onto a variety of canvases. The catastrophe of so many suicides is indicative of the inner tragedy endured by colourful people who simply could not bear to continue living in a grey world.

A more whimsical treatment of the same sort of issue can be seen in *Pleasantville* (1998), a film about two teenagers who get stuck in a 1950s black and white sitcom and can't help themselves introducing emotion to the people there. As people express emotions, so they turn from black and white into technicolour and find a fuller humanity in rejecting the conventional denial of part of their natural being. Yes, it is all a bit obvious, but it makes the point – albeit less subtly and movingly than *The Lives of Others*.

And this brings me back to Van Morrison and his brand new day. I feel I have had a very privileged life, not because I was born with a silver spoon in my mouth, but because I have been exposed to the arts as a natural and essential part of what is often called 'human flourishing'.

I cannot remember a time when I did not sing; but that is because I grew up in a church where we sang all the time. I might want now to question the content of some of what we sang, but the fact is that we sang. I then sang in a school choir and in school plays such as Shakespeare's *A Midsummer Night's Dream*. I started to play the trumpet when I was 11 years old and played in orchestras and a jazz group. I took up guitar when I was 16 and am still the only bishop I know who has been arrested for busking on the Paris Metro. (I was 19, working in Paris and ignorant of the licensing laws for buskers. I talked my way out of it and remained unscathed. They even let me keep the money.) I found myself listening to classical, jazz, big band, folk, rock and anything else recommended to me by more experienced and adventurous friends. Only opera and country & western passed me by, but even they caught up with me eventually.

I loved listening to singer-songwriters, learning to look through their eyes and loving the freedom from orthodoxies that allowed them (compelled them) to express their reality even when it was provisional, weird, silly, transient, contradictory or just plain mad. I discovered beauty in strange places and caught glimpses of God in the experiences and perceptions of some very unlikely people.

When I was a child I remember visiting the Walker Art Gallery in Liverpool and being totally bemused by paintings and sculptures that said nothing to me. This sort of art was a complete mystery and 'modern art' just seemed silly. When I lived in Germany I visited the Alte Pinakothek and the Neue Pinakothek in Munich and spent ages staring at the intense colours and thick substance of Van Gogh's *Sunflowers* – my first encounter with the man I had been introduced to by Don McLean's beautiful song *Vincent*. It was through this rather surprising route that I began to look at the Impressionist painters, and my move to Paris enabled me to spend every Sunday afternoon visiting a different gallery at the Louvre. In those days the Impressionists were housed in the Jeu de Paume at the end of the Tuileries gardens, close to the Place de la Concorde. My then fiancée's (now my wife) love of art meant that I could not avoid a greater exposure to a wider variety of art, but this only compounded my sense of ignorance.

When I was a curate in Kendal, Cumbria, Linda and I would go occasionally to Edinburgh, a city we still love to visit. On one summer visit we popped into the National Gallery of Modern Art and spent some time in an exhibition of artists such as Mondrian. I couldn't see the point of it all: a canvas with a black cross, three of the quarters painted yellow and one white – I could have done that. When we returned to Kendal I was being appropriately dismissive of this to a friend who happened to be an artist; he was surprised and rather cross. He told me that I was ignorant of the 'language' of art and shouldn't speak about what I clearly did not understand. When I remonstrated with him, he embarrassed me with the sort of blindingly obvious truth that I just had not seen: as a linguist I would not expect to learn Russian in a week, or to understand Russian literature simply by looking at it for the first time – it would take time and work to understand it. I was suitably chastised and his candour actually made me start to look at art with a bit more interest and humility.

Since then my wife has done further study in art and now practises as an artist using mainly glass and perspex. I love the galleries of London – particularly Tate Modern, but as much for the building and people-watching as the art itself. Nevertheless, the more I see, the more I realise just how ignorant I am and how philistine my reflexes are when confronted by 'new things'. The same is true of music. I can listen to anything, but I am still a creature of habit and love what I know. Despite one of my best friends being an international opera star, I still don't quite 'get it' and ballet leaves me cold. I love the sheer joy and fun of Jools Holland gigs at the Royal Albert Hall and I get to concerts by the Croydon Symphony Orchestra and Croydon Philharmonic Choir (of which I am a patron) whenever I can. Music feeds the soul in ways that cannot be articulated; it awakens emotions and thoughts that defy the restrictions of language.

I could argue similarly from literature and the stage. I have been an avid reader of books since I was a child. Because of my developing interest in languages I have been fortunate enough to be able to read literature in German, French and Russian as well as English. I have to confess to having been totally lost in a BBC Radio Russian version of *Chekhov's Uncle Vanya* and to making a fool of myself by always forgetting my words when I had a small part in a university production of Schiller's *Don Carlos* in German. But I was able to read some Lermontov, Turgenev, Tolstoy and Chekhov in Russian and I still read books in German, the language with which I am most comfortable. There is something wonderful about holding something solid like a book in which the author has shaped his or her thoughts into a journey which draws the reader on. Writers invite us into their world and try to help us to see through their eyes. They surprise us and comfort us as we look at a familiar world through unfamiliar eyes and find ourselves enriched by the imaginative excursions of someone we have never met. Books open up whole new worlds and have a power all of their own.

That is why films can rarely improve on the written word. In the same way that radio is said to evoke better pictures than television, so novels create imaginative space in which the mind can explore without being constrained by a fixed visual image. I still remember reading Jonathan Swift's *Gulliver's Travels* when I was 17 and realising it wasn't a child's story after all, but a deeply biting satirical swipe at the contemporary politics and politicians of Swift's day. Similarly, reading Alexander Solzhenitsyn in the 1970s and 1980s was more evocative of the horrors of the Soviet gulags than any news film or documentary could ever be. And it is this imaginative capacity of human beings that has to be kept alive and fed if we are to be truly human.

It should come as little surprise then that I believe the Bible needs to be taught to our children – not only for reasons to do with its content, but also because it embraces so many types of literature and drama, crying out for individual and corporate reading aloud. As any form of art embraces the untameable beauty and the raw horrors of human existence in a finite world, exploring the 'what ifs' of life, so the literature of the Bible reveals the heights and depths not just of individuals, but also of whole communities and countries. Its sweep is vast and its reach goes out to the farthest edges of the cosmos and in to the depths of the human heart. I will illustrate briefly.

This might sound a little bit controversial, but people who love the Bible can effectively shut it to people who have yet to discover it by pre-emptively declaring it to be 'the Word of God'. The judgement that it is 'the Word of God' should only be invited after the text has been read and understood, not beforehand; for to do so beforehand then constrains our reading of the text and it loses something of its power to surprise and challenge. Not to put too fine a point on it, if God has indeed inspired this written book, it is reasonable to assume that he intended its literary forms to be part of the communication. That is to say, poetry should be read as poetry, narrative as narrative, history as history, imaginative fiction as imaginative fiction. Contrary to the assumptions of some people, the text cannot simply be read off the page and understood without any effort or consideration of its form and wider context.

For example, Genesis chapters 1–11 is clearly Hebrew poetry and not scientific formula. When Isaiah says that 'the trees of the field will clap their hands', he does not expect us to throw the book in the bin because everybody knows that trees do not have hands with which to clap. The prophets were not people who simply got a supernatural message from God; they were people who knew the economics and politics of their day and saw behind them the inevitability of collapse if injustice was allowed to prevail unchallenged. Revelation is not a timetable for the end of the world, but a vivid pictorial account of the clash between, on the one hand, the empires that arrogate power and eventually drown in their own hubris, and, on the other hand, the

God who has shown himself in Jesus of Nazareth – and who in raising Jesus from death puts the power of the temporal empires into sharp relief. The gospels invite us to take a look at Jesus and decide who he is and how we account for what he said and did. When we read the Psalms we are supposed to give expression to the whole gamut of human emotion and experience – often when the particular words of a particular Psalm do not reflect our immediate situation, but must be expressed for when they do.

Now, I get irritated when supposedly intelligent people write the Bible off without having done the hard work of reading it and thinking about it. The Richard Dawkins and Christopher Hitchens of this world would rightly be horrified if I were to write off biological sciences on the grounds that Dr Mengele did some awful experiments in their interest. They would be justifiably annoyed if I were to avoid taking their writings seriously on the grounds that I had already written off their assumptions and therefore would be wasting my time reading them. They would legitimately ridicule any attempt by a non-scientist like me to question details of scientific method in obscure areas of research. So, why do they think they can dismiss the Bible (usually on the grounds that it depicts God as a monster) without having 'learned the language', done the reading and thinking, studied the texts? Why does one 'intellectual' rule apply to their disciplines, but be casually dismissed in the case of an inconvenient text? Should Shakespeare be dismissed without a glance simply because he belonged to a world which didn't look like ours? Richard Dawkins might be a great scientist, but he is not strong on texts, philosophy or theology.

But, lest I be accused of having a go at easy targets, the same questions need to be addressed to Christians like me. It does no service to God or the gospel for Christians to be illiterate when it comes to the Bible. The Bible has to be open to scrutiny and an intelligent reading – not simply to be squeezed through a filter that has been shaped by a pre-appropriated assumption about what it either says or should be made to say. Jesus noted this when (in John 5:39) he addressed people who were keen and committed religious people who studied their scriptures with diligence and integrity: 'You diligently study the Scriptures because you think that by them you possess eternal life. These are the Scriptures that testify about me, yet you refuse to come to me to have life.' Or, in other words: 'What you are looking for in all your close study of the Bible is actually standing in front of your nose – and you can't see it!' The gospels go on to demonstrate how it is the unlikely, undiligent, irreligious who recognise what is in front of their nose, whereas the diligent fundamentalists get Jesus nailed to a cross for reasons of blasphemy and embarrassment.

Once again, this brings us back to Van Morrison and his brand new day. The Bible's story is that the Creation itself speaks of God's character, constantly generating new life after death and decay. The new day dawns and brings with it new opportunities and the possibility of a new start. Our eyes are supposed to be opened to the beauty of what God has brought into evolving being and we should respond to this creation just as the Creator himself did when he stepped back at each stage of creation, looked at it and said, 'Wow! Isn't that brilliant?' The playfulness of the Creation narrative should encourage us to see God's creative activity as playful and joyful, not a labour of miserable duty. Our hearts should leap at a glimpse of the uncontainable glory of smells and sights and sounds that emanate from a world that smacks of what the English poet Gerard Manley Hopkins called 'God's grandeur'.

Some people will read this and think that I am being naïve because many people live in circumstances that keep their eyes fixed to the ground and reduce their horizons to mere daily survival. And they would have a point, were it not for the fact that even in such circumstances the human spirit cannot be totally suppressed. I remember walking around a dried up farm in Zimbabwe when there was no work for the people, the economy was in ruin, the water had run out and the fields were full of dead and rotting crops. People were hungry and there was real fear for the future. Then I came across a small circle of stones, no more than twenty centimetres in diameter. In the middle stood a single rose which had been watered. It stood there as a symbol of resistance to those who think that Robert Mugabe has the final word in this world – that defeat is the only possible outcome. It stood there as a reminder of hope, that there is colour in this grey world and God will not let himself be hidden. I have no idea who planted and watered that rose; but in that seemingly futile activity he or she is reflecting the God whose word is final: resurrection.

This is the radical hope that Christianity offers both individuals and communities. The women caught in adultery (John 8), the failed disciples such as Simon Peter, the men who deserted Jesus at the cross, Mary

Magdalene with her (legendary) dubious past: all these and more characters in the gospels found in their encounter with Jesus of Nazareth that their humanity was affirmed and their status as 'children of God' renewed. In the face of public suspicion and opposition from religious and political leaders, Jesus brought healing to the broken and offered a new life to people who had been told they were of no account in the eyes of both God and his people.

Go on into the story of the early Church (in The Acts of the Apostles) and you find the same phenomenon: people becoming Christians and finding their lives changed. They find themselves part of a community of people who love each other enough to share all they own with each other. They disregard the status symbols of their contemporary society and regard one another as equal in the sight of God and the Church. In fact, it was their tendency to forget just these things that led people like Paul to write to the Christian Church at Philippi (for example) to remind them of what distinguishes Christians from others. These people find new courage in retelling the story of God and people in a new way – a way that makes sense of Jesus, crucifixion and resurrection. These new Christians, who at Pentecost are thought to be drunk, find their human experience to be infused with colour and surprise to the extent that the world around could not help but notice.

Yet becoming Christian and belonging to a new community in which life took on a new dimension did not create some sort of trouble-free nirvana for them. Becoming Christian meant signing up for persecution, social disadvantage, misunderstanding and, in many cases, the need to flee their home and become refugees in other countries. Nevertheless, despite all the struggles, these people held to their new-found faith and changed the world by taking the Christian story, faith and values to a wider world that might not otherwise have been reached. What these Christians discovered was that finding themselves to be loved by God (as demonstrated in Jesus) demanded a response that relegated personal fulfilment or satisfaction to a rank below obedience to the God who loves eternally. That is why people would surrender their comfort, their security and their life for this God.

And this matters. The early Christians did not put their faith in schemas or formulae or timetables for the end of the world; rather, they put their trust in God and left the rest to him. Indeed, this is most visible in the book of Revelation where John, from his exile on the island of Patmos, urges the persecuted Christians to 'hold on in there', and not to give up. Empires come and go, he says. Power is transient and the powerful will pass away like the grass of the field and will one day have to meet their maker. In the face of this brutality and inhumane exercise of power by (in this case) the Roman Empire, hang on to God who in raising Jesus from the grave stole from them their arrogant power and mocked their apparent supremacy. The Empire might appear all-powerful and might snuff out your life in a cruel instant; but don't be taken in – God has the last word and it is 'resurrection'.

Two millennia of inspired art, music and literature have followed as Christians have explored the colourful depths of theology and what it means to be created, made in God's image, offered new life and hope, given a dimension of living that makes suffering and death bearable.

In one sense, Van Morrison continues in that tradition – whether he acknowledges it or not. The 'brand new day' brings new possibilities and new opportunities to shine fresh light into a sometimes dark world and to pour colour into what has been merely black and white and grey.

I have lived and worked in a variety of contexts in several countries and cultures. From big cities such as Liverpool, Bradford, Leicester, London and Paris to small towns and villages such as Cheltenham, Kendal, Rothley and Schwäbisch Gmünd, Christians find themselves in communities where they tell the same story of the good news of God in Jesus Christ. None are exempted from all that life can throw at them and some suffer more than others. But the inescapable fact remains that in all these places they work away not for their own benefit, but in order to help their communities flourish. Christians follow a God who did not opt out of suffering in the 'real' world, but opted into it – so, they do the same. Hence, the Church becomes a community that gives its life in order that others might find the colour of the kingdom of God; it aims to be a reflection of the Jesus we read about in the gospels.

At the beginning of the twenty-first century it sometimes seems as if the Church would prefer to spend its energies arguing about gender, ethics and the finer points of doctrine – often to the utter bemusement of an incredulous watching world. Perhaps we need fewer lawyers to manage the business of conflicting Christians and more poets to retell our story and renew our hearts with the old hope in a renewing God.

Chapter 9

WHAT IF GOD WAS
ONE OF US?

'What does God look like?' That is one of the
questions my elder son used to ask when
he was small and wanting to manipulate
the babysitter into letting him stay up longer. And it
wasn't only the babysitters; I would often find myself
succumbing to similar theological enquiries that were
clearly beautifully timed to cause maximum parental
anxiety. What if the question was actually genuine and
my refusal to address it turned out in the long run to be
the point where he left God behind? Well, it wasn't just
this question that he liked to come up with, but a whole
repertoire of similar theological conundrums designed
to delay bedtime.

What made this particular question a powerful one,
however, was that it is the fundamental question asked
by most of the world's great religions. What does God
look like? And how would we recognise him if we came
across him? And how can we possibly conceive of a
transcendent God looking like anything that we might
recognise anyway? If God is there, what is he/she/it like
and how can we know? So, you can see the problem I
and the babysitters faced in not knowing whether my
son was a genius asking the most profound questions
... or just being a clever nuisance. (Incidentally, he

didn't stop there, but went on to study philosophy at university.)

I have been involved since 2003 in an interfaith congress based in Kazakhstan. The initiative for the Congress of Leaders of World and Traditional Religions came from the President of Kazakhstan, Nursultan Nazarbayev, and the First Congress in September 2003 brought together leaders and representatives of a variety of world religions (including Christian, Muslim, Hindu, Jewish, Buddhist, Shinto and others) to discuss the need for inter-religious dialogue in a dangerous world. The reason the Kazakhs believed they had the credibility to host this encounter was straightforward: they had only been an independent state for twelve years and, despite holding together over 100 ethnic and multiple religious groups during volatile and vulnerable times of transition, they had defied expectations and had avoided internal religious strife. Located above the less stable southern republics of the former Soviet Union and, below them, Afghanistan, Iran and Iraq, Kazakhstan was positioning itself as the buffer state between east (China), west (Russia and Europe) and south (the 'Islamic' lands). Its political stability, growing economic strength, national self-confidence and religious coexistence provided a reasonable basis to offer the world a different sort of conversation.

There were many flaws to this concept and there are some religious groups who would not agree with the Kazakh President's representation of peaceful and equitable religious co-existence. The Hare Krishna community in Almaty, for example, was thrown off its own land in 2007, and despite international pressure to behave justly, the government offered the community some land (a fraction of the size of their own land) on a rubbish tip. There are other concerns about how minority faiths, including Christian denominations such as Baptists, are being treated – usually in relation to legal registration and taxation issues. In fact, moves to amend such laws are causing serious concern in mid 2008. These examples cast a shadow over the achievements wrought by the Congress and the reputation of the Kazakh government as one that deals equitably and openly with religious groups.

I worked on the Secretariat preparing for the Second Congress in September 2006 which involved politicians and representatives of the United Nations and the European Union. The Second Congress was charged with discussing 'Religion, society and international security' in the context of two themes: (1) 'Freedom of religion and recognition of others' and (2) 'the role of religious leaders in enhancing international security'. As with many such inter-religious dialogues, the Congress heard a lot of fairly anodyne speeches addressing the need for people of different faiths to talk together, and few addressed the themes themselves. Clearly, it is easier to talk about talking than it is to talk about substance. But, that said, it remains an initiative worth sticking with and developing.

For me, the most important and interesting element of such discussions is the opportunity to get inside the head of some of our interlocutors and try to look out through their eyes at God, the world and us. But that is where the whole thing becomes more problematic. For example, the Christians, Muslims and Jews all agreed on a draft statement that referred to the 'creation'. This proved to be a stumbling block for the Buddhists whose faith is monist and for whom there can be no creator because there is no creation. Getting round this proved difficult because the 'createdness' of the cosmos and its people is fundamental to the three great Abrahamic faiths. But, in the end, carefully chosen formulations of words were negotiated in order to allow a consensus to be expressed with integrity.

What I have learned (again) through these experiences – and they are ongoing – is that the 'the way the world is' looks very different when seen through the eyes of someone from a different culture who brings particular assumptions and prejudices to their worldview. And this is where the question of what God 'looks like' comes in. It is always risky to write in shorthand about any other faith, but I think it is fair to say that Muslims see God primarily and essentially as One who is to be obeyed in very particular ways. Buddhists would refuse to 'see' God at all in any 'separate' way. Jews will have a view of God and their own identity derived from their understanding of the Hebrew Scriptures in which God is so holy, even his name cannot be fully expressed. I don't wish to caricature these views of God, but merely to illustrate that even if we use the same word(s) to speak of the Supreme Being, we can mean very different things.

So, what I want to move on to is not a critique of how other faiths see God, but how Christians uniquely see God and what the implications of this might be. For the Christian answer to the question posed in Joan Osborne's great song (although it was written by Eric Bazalian) is that God was one of us. This audacious claim seems to many people to be utterly ridiculous, but it is the fundamentally unique feature of Christian belief and practice. We know what God looks like because he has been here among us in Jesus of Nazareth. But what does this mean?

For many people the Bible is a closed book simply because it is big, hard to get around and strange in its language and content. Sometimes preachers in churches assume too much and expound particular passages in detail without ever painting the bigger canvas onto which the detail fits. There are many succinct and pithy ways to summarise the big picture and I tried one out earlier in this book. But one way of understanding the Bible is to put it like this: if you want to know what God looks like, look at Jesus; if you want to know what Jesus looks like, read the gospels and look at us (the Christian Church). Now, that is scary. But it basically says that the story of the Christian scriptures is that God can be known and that we see what he is about when we look at Jesus. The Church, then, is supposed to be 'the body of Christ' – a tangible representation of what and whom we see in the Jesus of the gospels.

This is where the familiarity of the gospels to many people can sometimes prove a hindrance rather than a help. We bring to our reading or understanding of certain passages or sayings or events a set of filters which determine how we read and see. These are often not shaped by the text itself, but by impressions gained from elsewhere. These are often subconscious or even subliminal.

For example, every image you see in religious art and iconography of Mary the mother of Jesus depicts her as a slim young woman with a pale, sad face. Yet in John's account of the wedding at Cana in Galilee she must have been in her forties or fifties, a feisty woman who has endured widowhood and the hardships that are involved (John 2:1–11).

Or, was the child that Jesus 'put in the midst of his disciples' (Matthew 18:2–4) a boy or a girl – and was he or she 2 years old or 11 or somewhere in between? Was the child known to the people or related to one of them?

Was the woman with the haemorrhage a young, middle-aged or older woman (Mark 5:25–30)? Was she a beautiful, attractive 30-year-old (which is easily possible) or a sad and bitter 50-year-old?

I have always had a mental image of the woman who had been crippled for eighteen years (Luke 13:10–13) as an old crone. But she might have been in her twenties or thirties and have been otherwise beautiful.

Or, from the Old Testament, why do many people assume that when David killed Goliath (1 Samuel 17) he was a just a little boy? Goliath calls him a 'boy', but that is disparaging sarcasm aimed at scaring him. No mere 'boy' kills lions with his hands or carries armour for the king. He might have been a young man, but the connotations of 'boy' are misleading. We are told, for example, that the reason he couldn't face Goliath while wearing Saul's armour was not because the armour was too big or heavy for him, but rather because he wasn't used to wearing it (1 Samuel 17). So, how old was David?

We don't know the answers to these questions because the text doesn't tell us. But considering the questions can expose the prejudices we unconsciously bring to our reading of the texts.(Similarly, we don't know if the rich young man ever came back, having sold all his possessions (Matthew 19:16–22) or if Zacchaeus (Luke

19:1–10) ever gave up and went back to tax collecting for the occupation forces.)

I raise these questions here simply because our familiarity with the gospel stories in particular can blind us to the power of surprise and subversion we find in them. The danger we all face is that we shape the gospels in general and Jesus in particular in a way that makes us feel comfortable and fits a theological agenda we have already decided on from elsewhere. If I am honest, I think I grew up making the Jesus of the gospels fit a theology that was derived from Paul's letters – instead of the other way round. If the claim of the gospels is that they depict the Jesus who shows us what God looks like, then surely we must begin with them and let them stand for themselves. And we must take a broader look at the gospels in order to allow them to do their work in showing us Jesus.

I have written elsewhere about these matters (*Scandal of Grace*, 2008, and *Marking Time*, 2005), but will do a brief sketch here. This means taking an overview of Jesus in the gospels and not just extracting 'truths' from particular and/or disconnected passages.

What was Jesus Like?

'Jesus was born in Bethlehem' and that is a statement that already includes two startling facts. First, Jesus was born, came from inside his mother's womb after a pregnancy and was pushed into a dangerous and uncertain world – just like everyone else. In other words, God came among us as one of us and did not just explode into the world with a trumpet fanfare and all the power necessary to turn the world upside down. On the contrary, this baby was delivered into

155

a world in which survival could not be guaranteed and in which his vulnerability was precarious. High infant mortality rates, relative poverty and a context of military occupation by an arrogant yet paranoid Roman Empire were not the ideal conditions for God's intrusion into the mortal cosmos. Second, Bethlehem was a small settlement in an obscure part of the Roman Empire in a not-very-important part of the world (from the perspective of the colonialists). Yet it is here that Jesus was born.

The simple point here is that if this is the story of God coming among us as one of us, then it seems to be telling us that God is interested not in making grand gestures of power and glory, but rather in what Jesus would later refer to as 'a mustard seed' (Mark 4:30–2) – small, incognito and subject to all the world can throw at any of us. More than that, however, is the outrageous notion that God subjects himself to mortality, temporality and all the vagaries of human existence in a material world. When we easily recite the so-called Philippian hymn quoted by Paul in the second chapter of his letter to the Christians in Philippi we should stop and think through the implications of the shorthand summary: 'Christ Jesus, who, being in very nature God, did not consider equality with God something to be grasped, but made himself nothing, taking the very nature of a servant, being made in human likeness....'

Presumably, Jesus came back from exile with his parents in Egypt and grew up as did all children of his time and place. We must assume he had friends and that he had the same sort of relationships that growing children always have – including squabbles and fights through which we learn how to live together?

Presumably he went through adolescence and all the tensions that bodily and emotional change brings – and all at a time when his father died. His carpentry business must have meant that he had to deal with questions of profit and loss and all the other stuff that goes with making a living. Presumably his decision to leave all that behind and become an itinerant preacher was not taken in isolation, but in the face of opposition from his own mother and siblings.

Whom did Jesus Choose as Friends?

Jesus appears not to have been the best talent-spotter in the world. But he could only invite to accompany him on his travels those who were available to do so. This is part of what it means to be human and living in a particular place at a particular time. He could not conjure up a dream-team of super-disciples, but ended up calling a motley group of ordinary people who didn't even like each other. They also appear not to have been the brightest minds of their generation, being working men and women of diverse (and, sometimes, dodgy) backgrounds and histories. They were people who didn't understand what he was talking about and who held sad illusions about their own self-sufficiency and strength. One betrayed him, one denied knowing him and another doubted his identity.

Yet Jesus chose and worked with these people. We do not know if he invited anyone who declined the offer. What we do know is that Jesus did not favour religious 'keenies' or those with the most astute theological brains. He did not choose people who had got their lives sorted and who had nothing to hide. He does seem to have chosen people who probably wouldn't make it through an ordination selection process in most contemporary churches. Does this not suggest that Jesus has no illusions about the messy lives of those he calls to go with him, but that he calls people who can eventually be open to changing their mind about what God looks like?

Whom did Jesus Heal?

One of the remarkable things about Jesus is not that he healed people, but *which* people he healed. Take an overview and you see that he healed people who were considered 'unclean' or alien by the guardians of the faith. Untouchable people found that Jesus touched them; women who were ritually unclean found that Jesus welcomed them and did not regard himself as contaminated by them; outsiders and disliked people of dubious or questionable morality (like collaborating tax collectors) were given time and touch and an opportunity to be free; a woman caught in adultery was saved from a stoning and given a new life.

And what was the response of the religious authorities who saw themselves as the guardians of the true faith? Instead of celebrating the healing touch of God on broken lives, they got upset because Jesus broke religious conventions by making people well on the Sabbath. How is that for missing the point? Religious orthodoxy trumped the healing activity of God.

Who Embraced Jesus and Who Nailed Him?

Thus it was that the people who had a fixed view of 'what God looks like' and how God behaves came to the conclusion that Jesus must be punished and neutralised. It was people like me – the religious hierarchy – who got him nailed to a cross on a trumped-up charge on the spurious grounds that he was a blasphemer against God (who, they assumed, was more interested in rule-observance by legal pedants than he was in the end that the religion was supposed to commend: liberation and forgiveness and new life for all).

One of the best cinematic representations of this is to be seen in Denys Arcand's 1989 French-Canadian film *Jesus of Montreal*. An out-of-work actor is asked to modernise the Roman Catholic priest's decades-old Passion Play. Instead, he researches the story of Jesus and writes a totally new play which, in the end, is too difficult for the Church hierarchy to tolerate. It seems to question the veracity of elements of traditional Christian belief and takes Jesus's indictment of religious authorities a little too seriously. As the film progresses, real life becomes more and more like the story being depicted and, inevitably, it all ends up in tragedy. The film cops out at the end with resurrection associated with organ transplants (giving new life to other people around the world) – but, then, the revisionist academic research that underlies the play is embarrassingly feeble as well.

But the key thing about the film is the way the 'Jesus' figure (the actor collecting his theatre company) is a quiet, confident man who chooses very unlikely people to join him. One woman is sexually involved with the Catholic priest and also running a soup kitchen for poor, homeless people; one is doing voice-overs for a porn film; another is a beautiful model who is told by her showbiz producer boyfriend that she is just a body ... and will never be more than 'a great ass'. These people find in sharing their lives together a new community of love, respect and acceptance. It involves laughter and joy as well as fear, but it does not involve judgement by them on, for example, the hypocrisy of the priest. It evokes creativity as well as offence. Gospel events such as the 'temptations' of Jesus and the turning of the tables in the Temple are brought wonderfully to life. Filter out the nonsense and you find in this film a vivid and challenging depiction of Jesus and his frail friends: flawed, inconsistent, trusting, mixed-up and loyal.

How did Jesus Operate?

One of the surprising things about Jesus was his tendency to talk in stories and pictures. Whereas he sometimes spoke with his friends more specifically about what was likely to happen to them in the future, he usually taught in parables. The reason this is surprising is simply because it is easier to rule out ambiguity and enforce orthodoxy if 'teaching' comes in propositional statements. But, for example, Jesus never gave a three-line definition of the kingdom of God; rather, he threw out pictures and teased people's imaginations. As we noted in an earlier chapter, this is a dangerous way to keep people in line because the hearers might twist or deform the 'message' and then do things with it that the 'speaker' did not intend. Equally, however, the image or story itches away at the back of the mind and captures one's perceptions of what God is really all about.

I would venture to suggest that this is a contrast with the contemporary Church's obsession with getting people to sign statements and prove their orthodoxies by assenting to propositions that are framed in order to weed out those who do not quite conform. But didn't

Jesus say something about throwing the seed of the gospel wastefully all over the place and then precisely *not* pulling up the weeds that grow with the crops, but leaving that to God? Jesus can seem almost positively profligate with what we would call 'the gospel', sharing it with and giving it to the wrong sorts of people on the wrong days and in a rather casual way.

And the Church ... ?

Well, if I am right and the Church is called to incarnate (embody) the Jesus we read about in the gospels, then, presumably, people who encounter Christians should recognise something of this Jesus in them. I said earlier that this idea might be described as 'scary' and there is a good reason why. Look at the state of the Christian Church in the world – its schisms, conflicts, fantasies and corruptions – and the notion that we are 'the body of Christ' looks embarrassingly inappropriate. Surely, the Church should look like Jesus and bring healing instead of division, love instead of strife? But I would argue that the Church *is* the body of Christ and *does* look like his body. I will go on to explain what I mean by this.

Every time the Christian community celebrates its central act of worship – Holy Communion – it is making a bold statement and offering a counter-cultural invitation which many will see as a challenge. Almost the first thing we do in this celebration (called 'Eucharist', from the Greek meaning 'thanksgiving') is confess our failure and our need of God. It is one way of publicly disowning any pretence of self-sufficiency, arrogance or self-righteousness. 'We have failed – individually and collectively – and cannot proceed to worship God and

161

listen to him until we have faced our failure and owned up to it.'

We then go on to listen to 'the Word of the Lord' read from the Bible before being put in context and expounded in a sermon. Having heard that we are forgiven and given a new start, we are able to listen to God and try to understand how to live like and with God as we see him in Jesus.

In the light of this we then affirm our faith and bring our prayers to God before standing together and proclaiming in word and touch that 'we are one body' called to share God's peace despite our differences and conflicts. We should not go on to receive bread and wine while unaddressed tensions or unresolved conflicts remain between us. Only having exposed our fragility do we go on to rehearse our story and retell the story of what God has done in Jesus Christ to offer a new start within a 'being renewed' community.

Having verbally affirmed that: 'We are the body of Christ. Though we are many, we are one body because we all share in one bread', we have to move ourselves physically and kneel or stand with open, empty hands to receive what we can never claim, buy or demand. The bread and wine we receive becomes part of us, a physical evidence of what God is doing in and through us.

Having celebrated this gift of God, we are not then left to bask in the glory of God's generosity to 'me', but are sent out 'in the power of the Spirit to live and work to your praise and glory'. In other words, this act of worship is totally realistic about who and how we are as weak Christians in the real world and yet kicks us out back into that world to bear witness to this God we recognise in Jesus of Nazareth. This means we see ourselves summed up in the life, death and resurrection of Jesus – all three held together in our life and witness. For the world to look at the Christian Church is not to look at an image of perfection, but at a mess of wounds and unashamed exposure of those wounds to whoever wants to look.

Hypocrites are always welcome in the Church, but they will find hypocrisy itself exposed in the opening moments of worship when self-righteousness is knocked on the head by an open admission of failure. I would go so far as to say that the clamour for 'beauty' (understood as a single-minded orthodoxy in belief and unity) in the Church's image is a fantasy to be shunned and an idol to be spurned. The Church is a reminder to the world of brokenness – the broken and wounded body of Jesus himself – and that resurrection is not a form of escapism. The risen Jesus still bore wound marks in his raised body. The witness of the Christian community lies in being unafraid of its brokenness and reminding the world around that it too is broken and cannot hide for ever. The beginning of healing is to be found in a community that is realistic about the costs and contradictions of human living, a community that gives its life in order that the world around might find the courage to admit its own brokenness and find a welcome place among the 'being-healed' community.

This is why the Church should shun the sort of charlatans who promise health and wealth and prosperity if you get the formula right with God (which usually involves giving lots of money). Like Jesus, we can promise only a cross and self-denial; but we also offer a community in which we walk together and

163

talk together and pick one another up when we fall. We offer a community in which we can be open and generous, unafraid to acknowledge our weaknesses and failures. We provide a community in which people can lose their fear and drop their pride, and find a new dimension in human living. The symbol of the Christian Church is not a 'Victory' sign, but a cross – a gallows on which is hung a brutalised and exposed man whose world appears to have been defeated. We should not be ashamed of this.

However, this is not intended to justify failure and conflict in and between churches. On the contrary, admission of weakness and failure is the spur to humility in our dealings with one another. It is fascinating that Jesus sets the ethical bar quite high in some of his teaching, but then goes out and treats those who fall beneath it with grace, mercy and tender love. But the Church cannot hope to do the same while it shouts its claims to purity in such a way as to puff up its own image of self-righteousness and thus exclude those who know they won't be welcome.

And this brings us back to Joan Osborne and her vital question: what if God really was one of us? The Christian response is simple and clear: he is. The song goes on to ask what God's face would look like, if he had one. And we want to say, 'It looks like Jesus'. We have seen his face in Jesus of Nazareth and we are called to be a reflection of that face in our world.

Christians maintain that our looking at this Jesus gives us insights into all sorts of areas of human life. How Jesus treated people and maintained his own relationships shines some light on how we might reflect godliness in our own, for example. Relationships between men and women, friends and enemies, husbands and wives, children and adults, Christians and others, oppressed and oppressors: all these are touched on. But none of them absolve us of the responsibility to act and speak and live in such a way that the Jesus of the gospels is reflected in our ways of being. Jesus never forced his friends into behaving or believing as he wished them to do, but gave them the space and made them take responsibility for their own choices and decisions. He never seduced anyone into being a disciple, but put several off when he suspected that their motives were misguided or their will not strong enough.

I have been a Christian for several decades now and I have been through a variety of relationships with various churches. What I have learned is that it is far easier to criticise the Church for not being what I want it to be than it is to love the Church for what it is. But one of the most embarrassingly overlooked elements of the gospel narratives is the fact that Jesus called his diverse friends to walk with him and didn't give any of them a veto over who else could go. Their witness was to be worked out in *how* they lived together despite their differences, not in pretending to all be the same.

I have belonged to and worked with churches that organise differently, emphasise different features of theology or ecclesiology, embrace different forms of leadership and (I fear) proclaim different gospels. I have belonged to and worked with churches that handle the Biblical text in different ways and who have different understandings of what is going on when we worship. I have worshipped with churches that clearly think that God is either deaf or stupid and only wants to be praised and worshipped and reminded constantly of who he is. I have also worshipped with churches that shrink from any suggestion that God might want to be intimate with those he loves, embracing them in their difficult lives and loving them into self-acceptance. But – and this is the great privilege of being a bishop with oversight of dozens of parishes (in my case 102) – God is evidently at work in churches that sometimes seem to contradict each other. It would appear that God might be less fussy than his guardians when it comes to his choice of friends.

I began this chapter with a reference to the inter-faith initiative I am involved with in Central Asia. Rational argument is unlikely to move my colleagues into an acceptance of Christian faith; but I would hope that they might see in the Christians they meet something of the surprising and subversive touch of Jesus who claims to offer new life with the God who loves them to death and beyond.

Chapter 10

PILGRIM

One of my ambitions is to interview several great musicians about their life journey. Eric Clapton is at the top of the list alongside Bruce Cockburn. What I would like to know is how the worldview of these great artists has been shaped and changed by their experience of life and all it has thrown at them. And I would like to discover whether, now in their sixties, they feel they have settled into some sort of resolution to the conflicts that provoked some of their finest songs. 'Pilgrim' is a word that might be fairly applied to Clapton's life and search, not only to one of his most intense albums.

By contrast, my life seems to have been rather safe and routine. No drug addictions, no multiple relationship breakdowns, and far less travelling the world. But everyone has their own story to tell – even me. Mine would involve many features that would be hard to describe and of little interest to anyone else, but it is still necessary to try to put the story together somehow. For me it will involve the way learning other languages (German, Russian and French) and cultures has shaped the way I see the world, history and people. It will embrace people whom I have only met relatively briefly, but whose encounter has changed me. And I would have to recognise that many of the formative events in my life took place when I was a relatively young adult beginning to explore and experience the big wide world. I will offer an illustration of this.

I love Germany and Austria and I love the German language. I began to be interested in Germany when I was a teenager and had the opportunity to learn the language at school. I became intrigued not only by the events that led to the First and Second World Wars, but also how the country managed to rebuild itself after 1945. Since then, of course, the country has been divided for forty years and subsequently reunited. Prior to all this, though, the Reformation in Europe began in Germany, and the Germanic influence on music and art has been substantial. I became sufficiently interested in German politics to make it my main area of study at university. I have worked in Germany and Austria and have tried and failed to understand Swiss German.

In 2007 I took on the Anglican co-chairmanship of the Meissen Commission. The Meissen Declaration between the Church of England and the Evangelische Kirche in Deutschland (German Protestant Church) was agreed in 1988 and signed in 1991, thus setting the ground for closer relations and common partnership between the two Churches. Twenty years on the Commission meets regularly and pursues an agenda aimed at furthering our common witness and service in a fast-changing Europe and works to bring the Churches ever closer. The national committees meet three or four times a year and the whole Commission meets either in England or Germany once each year for a residential conference. The programme also includes further conferences, inter-church partnerships and theological cooperation. Being involved in this work has brought me into a greater involvement with Germany and some wonderful people.

I was over in Hamburg early in 2008 to promote a book that had been translated into German (*Speedbumps & Potholes: Looking for Signs of God in the Everyday*, 2004) as *Am Rande Bemerkt* (LVH, Hanover 2007), and used the opportunity to visit good friends in Hamburg. I gave in to the pressure to preach at my friends' church on the Sunday and was relieved when it was all over and the congregation seemed to have understood my limited German. During a walk later on we went into a bookshop and my friend mentioned a book that had taken Germany by storm following its publication in 2006: the diary of a television star who had decided to go on his own pilgrimage. I bought it and was not disappointed with the description by this reluctant pilgrim of the joys and traumas of his journey.

The author, Hape Kerkeling, is described on the cover as being 'Germany's most versatile television entertainer'. Among other things, he is a satirist and just the sort of person you wouldn't expect to do anything too serious without finding the funny side of it and then ridiculing it. So, when he published this journal of a 600-kilometre pilgrimage from a village in the French Pyrenees to Santiago de Compostela in Spain, many German eyebrows were raised. But it then turned out that he had not intended to publish his journal and had to be persuaded to do so. So, the book is a personal journal in which Kerkeling describes the experience as the most important journey of his life. Having come to an age and stage when his mortality seemed unavoidable (he had undergone major surgery), he decided to seek the meaning of life. In *Ich bin dann malweg: Meine Reise auf den Jakobsweg* (Malik, Piper Verlag GmbH, Munich 2006), he came to see his pilgrimage as both a challenge and an invitation – a journey that empties you and then fills you up again, that takes you apart and puts you together again differently.

Now, I have to be honest and say that he doesn't come to conclusions that I think necessarily hold water. But this personal account of this particular pilgrimage is not a pious résumé of holy thoughts by a holy man who sets out to get his prejudices confirmed or reinforced – rather, it is a warm, funny, honest account of an ordinary human being who knows that not every good thing in this life falls into the lap of the lazy. The thing about pilgrimage is that it is demanding and involves the deliberate leaving-behind of some of the props of life in order to clear the space for God to break in. Kerkeling embarked on his walk with faltering determination, very little luggage and a good sense of humour. But the journey was tough, full of surprising people and tested his seriousness time and time again.

But that is the point. Pilgrimages have always been for ordinary people who have decided to do something extraordinary in order to force themselves to walk with God, themselves and other people for a time. Just like the characters who walked together from Southwark to Canterbury in Chaucer's *Canterbury Tales*, everyone has a unique story to tell and a unique contribution to bring to the lives and experience of those they meet along the way. Every pilgrimage is unique and the end cannot be determined before the journey has been done. But, as Kerkeling shows us, it is worth the effort.

But pilgrimage is risky, too. It can be dangerous to leave behind the props and supports that give your life meaning and provide the security that makes life comprehensible. Pilgrims often find themselves transformed by what happens and by the people they meet on their journey, and unable simply to slip back into the life they had left behind. They often find they discover themselves to be loved and of value for who they are, not because of the status they have, the income they earn or the image they cultivate. Having left one life behind, you can't go back as if nothing has happened; life takes on a new dimension and finds a new depth of meaning and direction.

I know from my own experience that a pilgrimage is for ordinary people and is transformative. Earlier in this book I told briefly of my experience on the Scottish island of Iona and the life-changing impact it had on me. I could never replicate that journey and yet it shaped me and my ministry in ways that are hard to describe. But it was one of the most painful times of my life.

The journey by train from Bristol to Glasgow was awful and I missed the connection to Oban on the coast. I had to get a bus ticket and endure a three-hour sick-making drive along wiggly roads and all I could do was concentrate on not vomiting. I felt like death warmed up and dreaded the ferry journey on choppy seas from Oban to the Isle of Mull. After disembarking we then had to drive to the far south of the island on another coach before getting a second ferry to Iona where we had to walk to the abbey – vehicles cannot be taken onto the island (and there are no streetlights). What I haven't said thus far is that two of the things I loathe most in life are coach and boat travel. When we arrived at Iona Abbey we discovered that the heating system had broken down and that it was very cold on the edge of the Atlantic Ocean.

I have told something of this story earlier, but the point of referring to it again here is to illustrate that pilgrimage is not a holiday. It is costly because it involves the deliberate leaving behind of the things that bring us security and comfort, but it also might mean letting go of those prejudices and convictions that define who we think we are (and, by definition, who we think we are not). This happens because meeting and talking with others who are journeying from a different starting point (in themselves) challenges our preconceptions. And whereas in normal life there are plenty of distractions to help you avoid the hard self-questioning, there are none when you have travelled light and can do nothing other than live in the moment with whoever happens to be there with you.

However, you cannot sort of fall into pilgrimage in the same way as you might decide to stop at the pub on the way home from a concert. It has to be deliberately chosen and planned for. If it doesn't cost or demand anything, it probably isn't worth doing.

There are loads of examples of people who have gone on life-changing pilgrimages. These are not tacky devotional visits to dodgy religious sites, but sometimes involve spending time at places of significance in Christian history. For example, despite having avoided going on what I always feared would be a silly 'pilgrimage' to the places mentioned in the Bible, I still found myself moved when I did eventually go to Israel-Palestine and looked at Jerusalem from the Mount of Olives and recalled what had happened there two millennia before. Many Christians go on pilgrimage to holy places, as do Muslims on Haj to Mecca. It seems to be a human phenomenon rather than a specifically religious one that people throughout history have felt the need to leave where they are for a while and go to a place of spiritual significance seeking some sort of fulfilment. During the days of the officially atheistic Soviet Union, millions queued up for hours to see the embalmed corpse of Lenin in his mausoleum on Red Square – apparently, even atheists aren't exempt.

During the week I spent on Iona I also learned something else of enduring significance for me. Iona is called 'a thin place', a place where the veil between heaven and earth seems particularly thin and there is a mystical element to the atmosphere and environment. I was sceptical about this before I went and guessed it just meant it would be very cold and boring. Having been there and unable to escape from myself, my questions, other people (some of whom would not be my first choice for holiday companions) or the weather, I now understand what is meant by 'thin place'. But I also fear that many people I meet return from places such as Iona and want to take other people there to experience the same spiritual engagement. I think this is a mistake. Those who go there and experience the 'thinness' are called to go back to where they have come from and rub down the thick places until they become thinner. Simply to want to take other people to the holy place is to miss the point: Jesus refused to let his friends build memorial shrines on the mountain after his transfiguration and told them to get back down into real life and live it out.

What pilgrimages show is that God encounters people in very different ways and most people just go home eventually and get on with their life. They have been changed by the experience, but they have not usually turned into plaster saints for whom life has become a smooth ride to holiness. God does not turn us into clones, nor does he smooth out the humps and bumps of people's messy lives. It is perhaps inevitable, but still sad, that Christian books, magazines and agencies publish the stories of the people whose lives have been changed for the better by their newly found commitment to God through Jesus Christ, but don't publish the stories of those for whom life remains tough, God remains distant or life falls apart. This can then give the impression that getting the formula right (in terms of giving God what he wants in terms of devotion or behaviour) guarantees a good outcome. For most people reality is different.

I also want to recognise and celebrate the people who deny themselves the pilgrimage experience (whether real or 'inwards') in order to allow others to have it. The prime example of this is to be found in Mark's gospel (1:20) when Jesus invites James and John to leave their father's fishing business and go for a long, long walk with him and his other friends. It is easy to read the text and concentrate on the discipleship of the two brothers who leave behind their security and follow Jesus – a model of what it means and costs to be a Christian (apparently). But I wonder if we are also intended to consider their father, Zebedee.

Given the culture of the time and place where these characters lived, there is no way the brothers could or would have simply got up and left. They must have had

174

the permission of their father who would then have had to employ (at cost) others to take the places of the departed brothers. In other words, James and John could only fulfil their vocation because their dad paid the price. He didn't get to become a renowned 'super-Christian', but the brothers could not have done what they did without his almost anonymous generosity. Zebedee is also an example of costly discipleship – the one who makes it possible by his own work and sacrifice for others to do the higher-profile ministry and mission.

This leads me to wish that the stories of ordinary, routine, unspectacular Christian discipleship could be published and broadcast. Most people's experience of God is not exciting and dramatic; it is routine, sometimes full of doubt, and it involves 'just getting on with it', trusting that God knows and can cope with the messiness of it. But it is only the dramatic that really grabs people's attention and guarantees an audience. As someone once noted, 'Dog bites man' is not news – 'man bites dog' is. Unfortunately, however, the glory stories can give the impression that everybody ought to have a similar experience to those being reported and it can be disappointing to those whose experience is unremittingly just ordinary and routine and un-exciting.

This becomes clearer when we look at the Bible again. When reading the Biblical text we are in danger of losing time – literally. We read of events in several verses that actually took decades or longer. So, we speak glibly of the exodus of the Israelites from Egypt and forget the timeframes involved. The Israelite immigrants had been in Egypt for over 400 years before their liberation. But, just think what that means. If you had been born near the beginning of that time, you would have had a living memory (at least within your family or community) of past freedom. If you were born towards the end, as the crisis of persecution and slavery was coming to a head, you might have a hope of a brighter future in renewed freedom. But what if you were born 200 years into the captivity? No memory of past freedom and no expectation of future autonomy. You would have been subject to the temporal and contingent judgements made possible by events, context and the fact that no one had any idea of what was likely to happen next or how long this exile would last. Four hundred years is a very long time. What we read in a few verses as 'exodus' follows a huge number of days and nights during which the 'end' was unknown. What to us is 'past' was to them the unknown future.

The exodus did not resolve matters either. Over 400 years of exile was not followed by a great party and settlement in a lovely new home; instead, it was followed by forty years of wandering rather oddly through a desert while a whole generation of people died out. The people who easily romanticised the past were simply not able to be the builders of a new future with different challenges and opportunities. But this meant that families were bereaved and still the future looked uncertain. And it clearly made some of the refugees wonder if the whole 'exodus' thing had been a huge con.

I could make the same case about the exiles in the eighth and sixth centuries BC when the Jews were subject to the power of foreign empires. Seventy years does not sound much in a simple sentence, but try living the 25,567 days and nights (with allowance made for leap years) that make up those years – not knowing if and when or how the experience would be resolved. That puts it into perspective. For most people during those times life was probably unspectacular and they probably thought of their 'current' situation as the end of their world. They just got on with living as best they could with the memory of their God and their ancestors. We know little or nothing of the daily lives of ordinary people, but we do know that God knew and saw and noticed and responded to them.

The writer to the Hebrews puts it like this when referring to the ancient people of faith such as Abraham and Sarah: 'All these people were still living by faith when they died. They did not receive the things promised; they only saw them from a distance. And they admitted that they were strangers and pilgrims on the earth' (Hebrews 11:13).

In *The Pilgrim's Progress* (1678–84), John Bunyan recognises that we are all part of the pilgrimage of humanity and God's people, living our lives, doing our bit, but recognising that we will give way to others who in their turn will forget us and our part in shaping their world. Mr Valiant-for-Truth says:

> Though with great difficulty I am got hither, yet now I do not repent me of all the trouble I have been at to arrive where I am. My sword, I give to him that shall succeed me in my pilgrimage, and my courage and skill to him that can get it.

Pilgrimage demands the humility found by the recognition of what might be called 'meaningful transience'.

What the writer to the Hebrews refers to as 'the great cloud of witnesses' (Hebrews 12:1) will include a huge number of anonymous (both to us and their original contemporaries), ordinary people who just lived their lives as faithfully as they could manage and left the rest to the God in whom they falteringly trusted.

This will include the anonymous Jew who, hiding from the Gestapo, scribbled on the wall of a cellar in Cologne in 1942 these words:

> I believe in the sun though it is late in rising.
> I believe in love though it is absent.
> I believe in God though he is silent.

Timothy Ratcliffe begins his wonderful book *What is the Point of Being a Christian?* (Burns & Oates, 2005) with the verse of a song about pilgrimage and goes on to illustrate how pilgrimage is inextricably linked to hope. He identifies in the volume of people flying from place to place the kind of a human search for something like hope. He observes how the boundary between tourism and pilgrimage is a blurred one (p. 10). He recognises that pilgrimages can begin from deep convictions in some people, but also give space to those who are unsure and travel simply in the hope of finding something along the way. Pilgrimage is never a sign of despair, but ultimately and implicitly a sign of hope – born of a sense that life must be meaningful and that my life is going somewhere that matters.

But there is encouragement in all this, too. The Asian theologian Kosuke Koyama writes of how God himself goes on pilgrimage. In a theme to which he often returns in his meditations, he speaks of the slowness of God ... God goes so slowly that he even gets nailed to a cross in his search for us. Koyama suggests that we might also need to slow down in our approach to God.

Mike Riddell writes in *Godzone* (Lion, 1992) about the journey, the people, and their stories – three elements he regards as sacred. He tells a story of a man who tired of life and went in search of the Magical City. While camping for the night he left his shoes pointing towards his imagined destination. During the night someone turned his shoes round to point to where he had come from. In the morning he put them on and proceeded to the familiar place from where he had set out. But he returned differently because the journey itself had changed him. Riddell is illustrating that what he calls Godzone is not to be found in some fantasy place to which we can escape, but is to be discovered in the places where we are. Why? Because Godzone is where God is ... which means that nowhere is outside Godzone or beyond God's reach.

This takes us back to our ruminations on Mark 1:14–15 earlier in this book. When Jesus invites people to 'repent' and look at God, the world and themselves differently, he is telling them that God's presence is to be found here and now, while oppression continues under the heel of the Roman occupiers, and not simply in the resolution of their problems. And so it is that pilgrimage, however understood, is not an escape from reality, but a plunging us back into reality but with new and renewed hope, new and renewed perspectives, new and renewed relationships with co-travellers, and new and renewed vision for living the everyday life in the light of the one whose nature involves searching for us.

179

This is why I sometimes describe the job of the local church to be to create a place in which people can find that they have been found by the God who loves them.

Eric Clapton recognises the reality of pilgrimage when he sings of love and loss and the feeling that love has been wasted all these years. His beautiful and haunting song, *Pilgrim*, from the album of the same name, expresses the deep sadness of love lost and the lost bewilderment of someone who feels let down by the search for love. I think Clapton expresses better than anyone the inability of most people to avoid the search for love and the security of being wanted. His own pilgrimage, though not explicitly Christian, is worked out in his music and speaks at every turn of the reality of human loving and disappointment, the pain of rejection and the need to keep travelling and looking and wanting. In one sense this is the unavoidable outworking of what Augustine recognised when he said that 'our heart is restless till it finds its rest in [God]'. The honesty of Clapton's poetry is hauntingly impressive.

My own experience of being a Christian is not spectacular. I have had to learn to pray and to worship in different ways (and different languages). I have had to learn that the journey never ends in this life and that the conclusions I draw now are necessarily provisional. There are times of joy and contentment and times of frustration and spiritual aridity. Like everyone else, I struggle with myself and the weaknesses of my own character and personality, constantly wishing that God would make it all easier and just 'sort me out'. I persist in praying, but my understanding of what is going on in prayer has changed from 'telling God what I think he wants to hear' to 'trying to hear how God wants me to think and see' ... and then getting on with it. The spirituality I practise now bears little resemblance to that of my earlier experience.

What is crucial in all this is the fact that pilgrimage cannot be a solitary exercise. Pilgrims meet other people and are changed, encouraged and challenged by their encounters. Stories are told, insights are shared and time is spent in company with others who are at different stages of their individual and common journey. Although pilgrimage affects the person, it can never be a solitary or individual journey, lived in splendid isolation from other people. We travel in company with others who might both hurt and help us, make us laugh or weep. We cannot go it alone.

In Britain there is now a widespread rejection by many people of what they call 'religion'. By this they mean that institutional form of organised faith that seeks to control behaviour and belief, concentrating on what is wrong in life than what might be right. Instead, such people claim to be 'spiritual' – and spirituality has become an unthreatening word to describe that non-rational part of people's internal life (or soul). But it is also understood to be something private and to do with the individual, not something for a community. This is really questionable – owing as it does more to a sort of narcissism than it does to altruism.

But the sort of spirituality celebrated and encouraged by the Biblical narrative is always communal and never merely individualistic. For travelling in the company of those who have also been called by God to go on a journey to an unknown and uncertain destination demands resilience. Community demands commitment and comes at cost. In that sense I want to stand up for 'religion' and recognise that you cannot walk with God except in the company of God's people. Which is also why I believe in the Church and do not believe you can be a Christian 'on your own'. Pilgrimage is not just about what you get out of the journey, but also about what you contribute to those who accompany you or encounter you briefly.

I can only express immense gratitude to the people who have shaped my own spiritual journey. Some of them are mentioned in this book, but there are thousands who are not. I think of the Semraus in Schwäbisch Gmünd, the Türkis and Klaffenböck families in Traun, the Veiras in England, my family, clergy, colleagues, and so on. That is the privilege and challenge of pilgrimage: it involves an awful lot of moving and travelling and learning and growing and falling and thriving. In another great song with a terrible sentiment, the tragic Edith Piaf famously sang 'Je ne regrette rien' (I regret nothing); but most of us cannot say that with any degree of honesty. If you never regret, you never learn – and you are dishonest.

The Apostle Paul ended his angry and sarcastic (second) letter to the Christian Church at Corinth with an injunction that is used daily by Christians everywhere: 'May the grace of the Lord Jesus Christ, and the love of God, and the fellowship of the Holy Spirit be with you all.' This sums up what being a Christian is all about and should shape how we think of others who share our journey. The love of God is seen in the generosity of the Jesus we read about in the gospels; it is made real to us by the power of the Holy Spirit as we shape our life together in such a way as to resemble the Jesus we read about in the gospels. God who is relational commits us inescapably to relationship with one another – and that is where the joy and the challenge lie. It is also where the unique witness of the Church must lie, even if we fail a million times.

This book has been a sort of pilgrimage for me. It has picked up on a sort of 'soundtrack of my life', but has followed some of the twists and turns that have brought me to where I am now. I feel like an ordinary person whose journey has been messy, unpredictable, bewildering and mostly routine. I don't know where it will end or how or when. I have no idea if the book will have to be rewritten because future events will throw a different light on some of what I have related in here from the vantage point of my current experience. It is impossible to know the future, but pilgrimage is about keeping on keeping on regardless what is thrown at you. Hape Kerkeling began his pilgrimage to Santiago de Compostela with great resolve, but the weather on day one nearly defeated him. I have no illusions about my own fickleness and poor discipleship, but I trust in a God who is surprised by nothing and who promises to walk with me, come what may.

I look back through this book at musicians whose work has influenced me and accompanied me from childhood through adolescence into adulthood and mid-life. They remind me of the people I have met and the places I have been. I am reminded of the weaknesses and failures, but also of the lives that have been shared with mine and the privilege of serving communities through the Church. The role of a bishop in the Church of England involves a wide range of responsibilities and opens up a huge vista of opportunities. These include pastoral encounters and relationships, the exercise of leadership and administration, and the articulation of the good news of God on behalf of (and sometimes in spite of) the Church through a variety of means and media. The role involves national and international responsibilities and can be onerous as well as exciting. But I believe firmly that the primary duty of the bishop is to encourage people within and outside the formal institutions of the Church to open their eyes to the fact that the God who made them loves them, searches for them and sends them out to do the same in his name. He invites us to be found. And he lets it happen in different ways for different people at different times, and he will not be rushed.

In one sense, this book describes how I found faith. But that is not the end of the story because it illustrates that the journey of 'finding faith' never ends. It is not a destination; it is a journey, a pilgrimage. The faith I have found is real and continues to change my life and challenge my living, but it is lived out in the routines and challenges of everyday life in England. And it continues to be accompanied by great songs from all sorts of weird and wonderful people who have the skill to articulate in word and music the human search for the God who searches for us. Clapton sings about being a pilgrim for love, but the prayer for the continuing journey of faith can most beautifully be summarised from the plea of the great Bruce Cockburn: that the love that fuels the sun and creates the universe will keep even me burning.

Scandal of Grace

The Danger of Following Jesus

Nick Baines

978-0-7152-0866-3 · £8.99 · Paperback

'With insight and integrity, he shares a panoramic vision of the ministry of Jesus … His agility of mind, clarity of writing and refreshing insights make the book as much a companion to the Gospels as a commentary on them.'

John Bell, Iona Community

What was it like to live with Jesus? This is an inspiring exploration of what it means to live in the grace of God.

The friends of Jesus were not the sort of people that every leader would want to have around them. Their humanity was all too evident. They were people who had feet of clay, motives as mixed and fickle as fool's gold and relationship histories as colourful and patchy as a crocheted quilt. They were people like us – living with the outrageous grace and mercy of God among us.

Scandal of Grace is a revised and updated version of a title that was previously published by Saint Andrew Press as *Jesus and People Like Us*.

SAINT ANDREW PRESS

Marking Time

47 Reflections on Mark's Gospel for Lent, Holy Week and Easter

Nick Baines

978-0-7152-0829-8 · £5.99 · Paperback

'With insight and integrity, he shares a panoramic vision of the ministry of Jesus.'

John Bell, Iona Community

This book aims to help us reflect on God, Jesus and Christian Discipleship during Lent, Holy Week and Easter.

In what way is Jesus good news to each of us personally? What gives real meaning to the well-worn words 'good news'?

Straight-talking short reflections and prayers based on Mark's Gospel lead you through 47 days from Lent to Easter on a journey of real discovery. The author's pugnacious, pithy and vulnerably honest view of the key themes in Mark's Gospel will reveal the familiar through refreshed eyes.

SAINT ANDREW PRESS

Speedbumps & Potholes

Nick Baines

Introduction by Sarah Kennedy

978-0-7152-0806-9 · £8.99 · Paperback

'Thought-provoking with zest, careful reflection and great fun.'
Rev. Dr Richard A. Burridge, Dean of King's College, London

42 short and entertaining reflections come from observation and the ordinary, everyday experience and offer the reader glimpses of a new perspective on daily life.

'On a blustery cold day, as I write this, Nick Baines has worked his ecclesiastical magic and made me feel much sunnier. And that's a God-given gift'.

Sarah Kennedy, BBC Radio 2

SAINT ANDREW PRESS